EPHESIANS

Other Books by John K. McVay

*Seventh-day Adventist International
Bible Commentary—Ephesians* (forthcoming)

EPHESIANS
John K. McVay

Pacific Press®
Publishing Association
Nampa, Idaho | www.pacificpress.com

To order additional copies of this book or other Sabbath School companion books, call toll-free 1-800-765-6955, or visit AdventistBookCenter.com.

ISBN 978-0-8163-6692-7

January 2023

Contents

Preface

Ephesians should be read not only as a repository of truth to be mined for Bible studies and statements of faith but also as a dramatic account, as Timothy Gombis has argued, of a cosmic-scope story— God's actions in Christ in redeeming human beings and in creating the church as the special exhibit of His new plans for the human family. I hope that the chapters in this book, which provide a narrative commentary on segments of the letter, will help to draw you into Paul's drama as part of the body of Christ, the temple of God, the bride of Christ, and the peace-waging army of the Lord.

I am grateful to colleagues who have reflected with me on specific chapters: Andreas Beccai, Deirdre Benwell, Darold Bigger, Volker Henning, Pedrito Maynard-Reid, Steve Rose, and Ken Vyhmeister. I am especially thankful for two who have read every word: Larry Hiday and Pam McVay.

In writing this book, I have been keenly aware of the corps of teachers of the New Testament who have taught and mentored me: Frank Holbrook, Ron Springett, Ivan Blazen, Kenneth Strand, Abraham Terian, Nancy Vyhmeister, Sakae Kubo, Steve Thompson, Gail R.

O'Day, Douglas Parrott, Loveday Alexander, Andrew Lincoln, and especially, Ralph P. Martin. These amazing people have been gifts to me from the exalted Christ.

1

Paul and the Ephesians

Ephesians 1:1, 2; 6:21-24;
Acts 18:18; 19:41

How does Paul react as he walks the streets of Ephesus for the first time? Thanks to Luke's sketch of Paul's ministry in Athens (Acts 17:16–34), we have access to the apostle's mindset as he enters a city. Like many visitors, he walks the city's streets, inspects its buildings, and scrutinizes its public art (verses 22, 23). However, he is no run-of-the-mill, camera-toting, guidebook-carrying tourist. He is impelled by deep-seated convictions—a missional purpose burning in his heart. He examines the city from a specific point of view, wishing to understand its spiritual commitments. He is especially interested in the city's "objects of . . . worship," and among all the temples, idols, and altars, he watches for any hint of hunger for the one true Creator God (verse 23).

When Paul enters Ephesus, the city to which he will write the Epistle to the Ephesians (see the sidebar "Was Ephesians Written to Believers in Ephesus?"), he finds temples and shrines on every corner and block. These are mute witnesses to the idolatrous and syncretistic faith of the inhabitants of Ephesus, who worship every deity from A to Z: Aphrodite, Apollo, Asclepius, Athena, Augustus (the Roman emperor, worshiped as a god), the Cabiri, Concordia, Cybele, Demeter, Dionysus, Eros, . . . Pan, Paean,

Pluton, Poseidon, Roma, Serapis, Theos Hypsistos, Tyche Soteria, and Zeus.

Ephesus, located on the western coast of what we now know as Asia Minor, was at the intersection of the Cayster River and the Aegean

Was Ephesians written to believers in Ephesus?

Who first heard Ephesians read out loud in Christian worship? In Ephesians 1:1, the phrase "in Ephesus" (*en Ephesō*) is absent in early, important manuscripts, and some early church fathers were aware of a form of the text without the phrase. The words are included in modern Greek texts of the New Testament but are judged to be of doubtful authenticity.

However, omitting "in Ephesus" leaves behind a grammatical anomaly: the phrase "being also faithful" (*tois ousin kai pistois*) becomes clumsy in Greek and the participle "being" (*ousin*) is used without a predicate, going against Paul's usual practice (Romans 1:7; Philippians 1:1; cf. 1 Corinthians 1:2; 2 Corinthians 1:1). Moreover, the presence of "in Ephesus" has significant support among the manuscripts. Even the manuscripts that delete "in Ephesus" include the letter's title—PROS EPHESIOUS ("To the Ephesians")—leaving no direct evidence the letter circulated without being identified with Ephesus.

In this light, it is best to affirm that our epistle is, indeed, "The Epistle to the Ephesians," written by Paul to believers in Ephesus. However, Paul addresses a very different church than the one he had left behind several years earlier. The letter treats broad themes but offers few local details. This suggests that Paul composed it to be read in the various house churches that had sprung up in greater Ephesus and in the network of congregations established in the region.

Sea. At the time of Paul, it was the "mother city" and capital of the Roman province of Asia, one of the richest regions of the Roman Empire. It had a population of 200,000 to 250,000, making it the third- or fourth-largest city in the empire. As a major port city, Ephesus was also a transportation hub for inland traffic. Attracting residents from Anatolia (Asia Minor), Greece, Egypt, and Rome, it was a cosmopolitan and multiethnic city with a longstanding Jewish population of significant size. The city boasted many amenities, including spacious streets and stoas (covered, colonnaded walkways), commercial and state agoras (marketplace complexes), gymnasiums (athletic training facilities), a stadium (used for chariot races and other events), the *Prytaneion* (the town hall, which doubled as a worship center), public baths and toilets, and a large amphitheater seating twenty-four thousand (the venue for theatrical performances as well as religious, civic, and athletic events).

Touring the city during his first brief visit (Acts 18:18–21), Paul would have seen that the Ephesians reserved a special place of honor for the goddess Artemis. "Artemis of the Ephesians" (Acts 19:28; a modified version of the earlier Greek goddess Artemis and the Roman Diana) dominated the politics, culture, and economy of Ephesus, and the city was the center of her widespread cult. Her richly decorated temple, the *Artemision* (verses 23–41), was located outside the city walls. As the largest temple in antiquity, it was one of the seven wonders of the ancient world. The Artemision served as the major banking center for the region and was the starting and ending point for biweekly, circuitous processions that featured images of Artemis. Coins displayed her image, and regular athletic games—the *Artemisia*—were conducted in her honor. Her birth was celebrated elaborately each year, and a month of the year (roughly corresponding to April) was named after her.

Artemis was worshiped in complex worship rituals at the Artemision as "Queen of the Cosmos," "heavenly God," "Lord," and "Savior," who controlled heaven, the earth, the underworld, and the spirits who inhabited them. Statues show her in an elaborate costume, presenting various symbols of the power she offered to worshipers. She wears the zodiac as a necklace or garland, symbolizing power over the supernatural and astrological powers that determine fate. She also wears a tight skirt featuring heads or busts of real and mythical animals, announcing her power over animals and demons. Much-discussed rows of bulbous objects across her chest are probably not breasts, as has often been assumed. They may represent eggs, steer testicles, armor, or small leather bags filled with magical words (the "Ephesians letters" or *Ephesia Grammata*) that were believed to offer spiritual power and protection. She was adored as the guardian and protector of the city and its citizens.

Against this backdrop, Paul's initial visit triggers his dream of a transformed worship horizon for Ephesus, one in which the worship of the Lord Jesus Christ monopolizes the allegiance of the city's inhabitants. He imagines a new society—the church—planted, growing, and transforming the city. Believers, shaping their lives after the self-sacrificing Jesus, introduce a new, love-empowered ethic and a fresh pattern of human thriving.

When Paul returns to Ephesus, he goes to work to actualize that vision. He begins in his usual place, the synagogue, where he "argues" for three months (Acts 19:8). When he is ejected, he rents the lecture hall of Tyrannus (verse 9; "the Tyrant," a nickname doubtlessly pinned on him by his pupils!). Paul begins his days making leather goods and tents. Then, during the hottest part of the day, when many would be available to attend, he walks to the lecture hall, where he teaches and mentors emerging believers. "This continued for two years, so that all the residents of Asia heard the word of the Lord, both Jews and Greeks" (verse 10).

During this time, "God was doing extraordinary miracles by the hands of Paul, so that even handkerchiefs or aprons that had touched his skin were carried away to the sick, and their diseases left them and the evil spirits came out of them" (verses 11, 12). One of the most widely worshiped gods in the Greco-Roman world was the Greek god of healing, Asclepius.

Paul and the Ephesians

Ephesus had its *Asclepion*—its temple to Asclepius. Such temples were places of worship, but they also served as health clubs and restaurants; social centers that provided access to influential people. The sick would come and pray to Asclepius for healing. They would make vows to the god, and if healed, they would return, bringing a terra cotta image of the healed part and leaving it in payment of a vow. Now, in the dining halls and baths of the Asclepion, the talk is not about the powers of Asclepius. The talk is about a man named Paul and the God he serves. The coffers of Asclepius begin to dry up, but there is a run on sweat rags and work aprons!

In Ephesus, there was a group of wily, streetwise Jews who had taken advantage of the reputation of their faith. The Bible calls them "itinerant Jewish exorcists" (verse 13). For a price, they would rattle off long, complicated chants that invoked every deity from A to Z. The rewards must have been quite handsome, for seven sons of a self-styled "high priest" named Sceva all took up the occupation. Alert to trends in religious belief, they wished to remain on the cutting edge of their craft. Their income depended on pleasing their customers. So, when they heard the names "Paul" and "Jesus" being spoken in honorific tones, they penciled them in among their incantations.

With their freshly adapted abracadabra, their newly formulated mumbo jumbo, they make a house call on a demon-possessed man: "Then some of the itinerant Jewish exorcists undertook to invoke the name of the Lord Jesus over those who had evil spirits, saying, 'I adjure you by the Jesus whom Paul proclaims.' . . . But the evil spirit answered them, 'Jesus I know, and Paul I recognize, but who are you?' " (verses 13, 15). Now, you must admit this is a creative evangelistic strategy! In place of polished media presentations and neatly groomed evangelists, you have seven naked, wounded men running through the streets. The strategy is as successful as it is strange: "And this became known to all the residents of Ephesus, both Jews and Greeks. And fear fell upon them all, and the name of the Lord Jesus was extolled" (verse 17). Here is a deity who will tolerate no rival. Here is a God who knows no peer. Here is a jealous God who refuses to relinquish the unique claim of His love upon His creatures.

Of all the fascinating twists and turns in the story of Paul's ministry in Ephesus, the next few lines are especially riveting. But you must read them closely: "Many of those who had come to faith came forward to confess and admit their practices. Quite a few of those who practiced magic gathered their books together and burned them in public. The value of these books was assessed to be 50,000 silver coins."[1] These were people who had become Christians—to a certain extent. They confessed Jesus Christ as *a* lord and *a* savior. They said their prayers to Christ *and* chanted their spells. They knelt at the foot of an old rugged cross *and* wore talismans. They managed their lives with the wisdom of Scripture *and* the gibberish of their manuals of magic.

The sight of seven naked, wounded, panic-stricken men fleeing through the streets proved a unique tonic for their ailing spirituality. These quasi believers recognized that they shared a common flaw with the seven sons of Sceva. They had honored the name of Jesus with all the rest. They had mingled their devotion to Christ with their practice of magic. But there could be no question that now they became fully devoted to the risen Lord. Into the bonfire went their pricey magic manuals, worth fifty thousand silver coins. Since a silver coin was a working man's pay for one day, this would represent a vast sum. The gods of Ephesus had fallen. Even the gods of riches, fortune, and materialism had bowed the knee.

The backstory of the Epistle to the Ephesians—the stories we reviewed in Acts 19—is a prequel to the letter itself. We are introduced not only to important history but also to the theological infrastructure of the letter. Its great themes—that Jesus, exalted over every power and name, created the church to exhibit His reconciling, unifying power—occur in Acts 19 in compelling story form. We watch as the economy and politics of a large, sophisticated city are jolted by the story of Jesus. We watch as lives are transformed.

Paul and the Ephesians

* * * * *

I had tried them all. I had placed my offerings upon the altar of Eros. I had offered my sodden praise before the statue of Dionysus. I had participated in the mysteries of Cybele, the "Great Mother," descending into her underground pit, the blood of a slain bull dripping on me, intended to give me access to Cybele's cosmic power. However, each new experience, pilgrimage, sacrifice, feast, and ceremony ends the same way: I return to look into my Corinthian mirror, and I see the same sad sight—hollow eyes mirroring a hollow heart.

Demetrius is good to me, setting up shop for me on a major thoroughfare to Artemis's grand temple, selling our city's trademark souvenir—small, silver shrines to Artemis. When things get a bit slack, he speaks a quiet word to a tour leader or two, and soon, I have all the business I need.

However, there comes a time when sales drop off precipitously. Even Demetrius cannot improve my sagging profits. He calls an emergency meeting of the manufacturers and sellers of the trinkets of Artemis and gives this speech: "Men, you know that we get our wealth from this business. You also see and hear that not only in Ephesus but in almost the whole of Asia this Paul has persuaded and drawn away a considerable number of people by saying that gods made with hands are not gods. And there is danger not only that this trade of ours may come into disrepute but also that the temple of the great goddess Artemis will be scorned, and she will be deprived of her majesty that brought all Asia and the world to worship her" (verses 25–27, NRSV).

In response, we all start to shout, "Great is Artemis of the Ephesians!" Almost instantaneously, this draws a huge crowd that charges its way to the amphitheater, dragging along two of Paul's helpers, Gaius and Aristarchus. There, the shouting continues for two hours: "Great is Artemis of the Ephesians!"

When the town clerk disperses us, I return home to rub a very sore throat and look deeply into my Corinthian mirror. As I see my own worried brow again, I recall Gaius and Aristarchus. There had been a determination in their faces, a fresh sense of purpose. I know that I must find them. So when darkness falls, I make my way through the streets of the city. I ask here and there, and eventually, I am ushered into a room where those two are nursing their wounds of the day.

I am not coy in my request. I blurt it out: "The purpose, the decision, and the joy that I see on your faces, how do I get them?"

The next few hours are the most incredible of my life. I learn that there is a God who loves me and calls me to worship His Son. I am not called to worship God and anyone or anything else. I am called to bow the knee before only One and to serve Him alone.

The next morning I know what I have to do. I find Demetrius. I thank him for all he has done for me, and then I pull the shop keys out of my pocket and hold them out to him. His face flushes. He asks me what in the cosmos I am doing. Quickly, I stutter out the message that I can no longer sell the shrines of Artemis. As his anger boils, I drop the keys and run.

For the first time in a long time, I have no clue where my next meal is coming from. But as I run from Demetrius, I feel it spread across my face—that wide and joyful smile.

* * * * *

If the risen Lord Jesus showed up on the sidewalks of your hometown as obviously as He did in the streets of Ephesus, what industries would go belly up? What trinkets would go unsold? What temples would go begging for pilgrims? Who would demand a meeting in the amphitheater? What deep, gnawing needs of human hearts would be met? What would happen if, once again, the gods came tumbling down?

---

1. Eckhard Schnabel, *Acts*, Exegetical Commentary on the New Testament (Grand Rapids, MI: Zondervan, 2012), 776; verses 18, 19.

2

God's Grand, Christ-Centered Plan

Ephesians 1:3-14

It is a startling invitation: "Come up here!" Instantly, John the revelator finds himself before the throne of God. Amid flashing lightning, growling thunder, and blazing torches, John hears the hymn of four impressive creatures, which cues the worship of twenty-four elders, who fall from their thrones, prostrating themselves before the One seated on *the* throne. In prone worship, they send their crowns skittering across the glassy, icelike sea toward God's throne as they begin their worship of the Creator:

> "Worthy are you, our Lord and God,
>   to receive glory and honor and power,
> for you created all things,
>   and by your will they existed and were created" (Revelation
>   4:11).

A call to just that kind of worship is how Paul opens Ephesians. In Ephesians 1:3–14, he draws believers into "the heavenly places" (verse 3), to God's cosmic throne room and the initiatives of His grace anchored there. Before that awe-inspiring throne, we listen, agape, to the ageless dreams and plans God has for us. Hearing those plans, we fall before the throne and send our crowns skating across the crystalline sea. We join in worshiping the Father-Creator of us all.

Worship

Paul writes his letter to be read out loud to gathered members of early house churches in Ephesus as an integral part of their Sabbath worship. So, in Ephesians 1:3–14, he begins with an intense call to worship. In Greek, the passage constitutes one very long and complicated sentence. Classics scholar Eduard Norden called it "the most monstrous sentence conglomeration . . . I have ever met in the Greek language."[1] Eugene Peterson replies, "Christians who hear or read this sentence in the company of a worshiping congregation are likely to dismiss the fussy grammarian's outrage as a whimpering whine. Who can resist this marvelous, tumbling cataract of poetry?"[2]

Ephesians 1:3–14 is the start of something big in the epistle, which exhibits the highest concentration of prayer and worship language of all Paul's letters. Paul includes the following types of prayer and worship passages in Ephesians:

- *Prayer benediction.* A prayer blessing inviting God's blessing on believers: "Grace to you and peace from God our Father and the Lord Jesus Christ" (verse 2).
- *Praise benediction.* A prayer blessing that "blesses" God: "Blessed be the God and Father of our Lord Jesus Christ, who has blessed us in Christ" (verse 3).
- *Doxology.* A specific type of praise benediction, attributing glory to God: "To him [God the Father] be glory in the church and in Christ Jesus throughout all generations, forever and ever. Amen" (Ephesians 3:21).
- *Prayer report.* Paul reports how he prays for believers: "I do not

cease to give thanks for you, remembering you in my prayers" (Ephesians 1:16).

Paul includes these different types of worship passages in Ephesians, together with exhortations to participate in worship and prayer, as seen in table 1.

Table 1. Worship, prayer, and praise passages in Ephesians

Passage from the book of Ephesians	Type of literature	Description
Chapter 1:2	Brief prayer benediction	"Grace to you and peace from God our Father and the Lord Jesus Christ."
Verses 3–14	Lengthy praise benediction	Blesses God for the blessings offered to believers in Christ through the Spirit.
Verses 15–23	Prayer report	Reports Paul's prayers for believers, inviting the Father to give them the Spirit, who actualizes the power of the risen and exalted Jesus.
Chapter 3:14–19	Prayer report	Reports Paul's prayers for believers, asking the Father to grant inner strength through the Spirit.
Verses 20, 21	Doxology	Celebrates God's glory in the church and in Christ.
Chapter 5:3, 4, 18–21	Exhortation	Exhorts believers to gather and share in pure, Spirit-filled worship.
Chapter 6:18–20	Exhortation	Exhorts believers to practice regular prayer "in the Spirit" for all the saints and for Paul.
Verses 23, 24	Two brief prayer benedictions	Invokes God's peace, love, faith, and grace to rest on believers.

When we consider how central worship is to the Epistle to the Ephesians, we are justified in taking it as a textbook on worship, with Ephesians 1:3–14 as its first chapter.

The why of worship: Who God is

Ephesians 1:3–14 teaches us that we worship God for who He is. God is a God of love who loves us as His children (verse 5). God does not express His love stingily but lavishly (verse 8). It is the generous, gracious triune God who loves us because the Father (verses 3–6), the Son, our Lord Jesus Christ (verses 7–12), and the Holy Spirit (verses 13, 14) are all active participants in our salvation.

However, the language Ephesians 1:3–14 uses about God's decision-making concerning believers presents us with a significant challenge: "chose us in him before the foundation of the world" (verse 4), "predestined us" (verse 5), and "having been predestined" (verse 11). This passage is often considered one of the classic places in Scripture where a Calvinist doctrine of divine predestination is taught.[3] For example, in the Westminster Confession of 1647, chapter 3, sections 3 and 4 say, "By the decree of God, for the manifestation of his glory, some men and angels are predestinated unto everlasting life, and others foreordained to everlasting death. These angels and men, thus predestinated and foreordained, are particularly and unchangeably designed; and their number is so certain and definite that it can not be either increased or diminished."[4] Does such a view accurately reflect the thought of the passage itself? Or is it imposed on Ephesians 1:3–14?

We must identify with Paul's original audience as we consider ideas of election and predestination in Ephesians 1:3–14. Unlike members of democratic societies today, the Ephesians had no sense that they could decide their own destiny or fate. Rather, they believed that their destinies had already been fixed through the power of the stars and planets. "Oriental astrology and occultism . . . with [their] . . . accompanying astral religion and dominant fatalism, haunted like a nightmare the soul of first-century people. . . . People who came under the spell of star worship were made to feel that all things were ruled by 'fate.' The particular conjunction of the stars or planets under which people were born was of decisive importance and settled irretrievably their destiny."[5]

When those first-century people heard the gospel, it came to them as very good news. Their lives were not in the hands of chance and fate. Their destinies were not determined by astral powers. Instead, God offered them eternal life through Jesus Christ, who, above any competing power, was now the Lord of their lives.

Working carefully through Ephesians 1:3–14, we discover that Christ is mentioned six times by name, title, or description and by a pronoun an additional seven times. Of these thirteen mentions of Christ, eleven are preceded by the preposition "in." In this Christ-saturated passage, Paul repeatedly affirms that when believers exercise Spirit-motivated faith in Christ (verses 12, 13; cf. Ephesians 2:8, 9; 4:21; 5:14; 6:23, 24), God then considers them to be "in Christ." At that moment, His destiny becomes their destiny, and "every spiritual blessing in the heavenly places" (Ephesians 1:3) becomes theirs.

This explains why the decision to exercise faith in Christ is exceptionally important to Paul in Ephesians and why he repeatedly rehearses that event in the lives of his addressees. Ephesians 1:3–14 is the first and foundational rehearsal of their conversion. Paul first describes at length the rich array of Spirit-induced blessings triggered at that moment (verses 3–11). Then he celebrates the transforming moment itself (verses 12–14). Like Paul and other believers before them, who hoped in Christ (verse 12), they "heard the word of truth, the gospel of . . . salvation" and then believed in Christ (verse 13).

In the prayer report that follows (verses 15–23), Paul reviews their conversion again, rejoicing in the time when they came to "faith in the Lord Jesus" (verse 15) before praying that the Spirit-mediated blessings released by trusting in Christ might be richly present in their lives (verses 16–23). In Ephesians 2:1–10, Paul will yet again narrate their conversion, marking when they came to Christ "through faith" (verse 8).

From a broader history-of-salvation perspective, he tells again the story of their conversion in verses 11–22, reflecting on it as the time when Christ Himself "preached peace" to them (verse 17). In Ephesians 3:1–13, he evokes their decision for Christ by accenting his own role to "preach to the Gentiles the unsearchable riches of Christ" (verse 8). In his second prayer report (verses 14–19), he records his prayer that their faith commitment to Christ might result in rich, spiritual lives: "that Christ may dwell in your hearts through faith" (verse 17).

In Ephesians 1:3–14, Paul sets the pattern for emphasizing conversion and faith by repeating again and again that spiritual blessings are bestowed and actualized "in Christ." In advance, in deep time, God crafted a response to the incursion of Satan and sin (Ephesians 2:1–3), opening up a whole new pattern for human thriving—the plan of redemption in Christ (Ephesians 1:7), which is activated for the addressees when they hear of that plan and believe in its Hero, Christ.

Drawing these two points together—the first-century context of astral religion and the importance for Paul of exercising faith in Christ—provides an important response to a Calvinist (predestination) view of the passage. Converts to Christ are reminded in Ephesians that God is not the fatalistic taskmaster they knew in the astral powers, decreeing for them a predetermined future they did not choose and cannot avoid. Rather, in Christ, they worship God as One who offers them new trajectories for the future and invites their free choice, encouraging them to respond in faith (verses 13; 3:17). "This is a rescue from impersonal fate, from astrological charts, from karma and kismet, from 'biology is destiny.' "[6]

The why of worship: What God does

We worship God for *who He is* and *what He does*. Paul's call to worship in Ephesians 1:3–14 invites us to worship God for His abundant blessings upon us when we believe. Eight verbs employed in the passage summarize the grand variety of God's work for believers:

1. In the opening, overarching statement, God *blesses* believers (us!) with "every spiritual blessing in the heavenly realms in Christ" (verse 3, NET).

2. In Christ, God *chooses* believers to be "holy and blameless before him" (verse 4; cf. verse 11). We stand before Him justified by His grace, offered to us in Jesus.

3. Through Jesus Christ, God *destines* us. This is no sterile, legal relationship because we are adopted as His children (verse 5).

4. "In the Beloved"—that is, in Christ—He *gives* us "his glorious grace" (verse 6; or "graced us with his glorious grace," since in Greek, the verb and noun are related).

5. In Christ, God *lavishes* upon us a whole set of treasured spiritual blessings: "redemption through his [Christ's] blood, the forgiveness of our trespasses, according to the riches of his [God's] grace" (verse 7). Note that the final phrase highlights afresh the abundance accented in the verb "lavished" (verse 8). "In matters of God's grace, hyperboles are understatements."[7]

6. God *makes known* to us all this "mystery of his will" and His "purpose," which He exhibits in Christ (verse 9). If God's grand plans and blessings remained unknown to us, they would do us no good. His revelation of the gospel is among His greatest blessings to us.

7. God's actions to redeem us are part of His grand, cosmic plan for the future, though one that is already underway in the present. In His "plan for the fullness of time," God *heads up* "all things in him [Christ], things in heaven and things on earth" (verse 10).

8. At their conversion, God *seals* believers with the Holy Spirit (note that the verb is stated in the passive: believers "were sealed with the promised Holy Spirit," verse 13). The Spirit is both a "seal" upon believers (because a seal is a sign of ownership) and the "guarantee" or "down payment" of still fuller blessings reserved for believers in the future (verses 13, 14).

Note the mention of "every *spiritual* blessing" at the beginning of the passage (verse 3; emphasis added)—with the adjective "spiritual" (Greek, *pneumatikos*) suggesting that these blessings come through the Spirit (*pneuma*)—and the announcement of the Spirit as seal and down payment at the end (verses 13, 14). For Paul, the presence of the Holy Spirit in believers' lives is the grandest blessing of all (Ephesians 1:16–23; 3:14–19).

What is notable about the verbs in Ephesians 1:3–14 is that they all describe God's actions. This passage invites us to join believers across the ages in accepting all God's blessings and praising Him for them. However, these acts of faith and praise are not native to human beings who are "dead in trespasses and sins" and "by nature children of wrath" (Ephesians 2:1, 3). Paul will remind us that salvation—and faith as well—is "not of your own doing" but is "the gift of God" (verse 8). All of God's blessings, including the faith in our hearts and the praise of God on our lips, are ours only in Christ. God lavishes the riches of His grace upon us in our spiritual bankruptcy. All is of grace! Celebrating the grand news of the gospel, we participate in elevated worship as we join the heavenly hosts in the cry, "Worthy is the Lamb who was slain!" (Revelation 5:12).

* * * * *

The worship service is being held secretly in a forested corner of Italy's northern Alps. Beginning late in the evening, it exhibits none of the usual trappings of the worship of the time—no priest, no altar, no vestments, and no complex liturgy. The interest is high, so the little group extends their study and worship long into the night. The service is housed in a remote, dilapidated, and unheated cabin, with the light of a single candle illuminating a few precious pages of Scripture laid out on a rough table. An artisan quizzes the Waldensian duo who have been reading the Bible's teaching about the gospel: "Will God indeed accept my offering? Will He smile upon me? Will He pardon me?"

Reaching for a page from Matthew's Gospel, one of the Waldensian missionaries reads, "Come to me, all who labor and are heavy laden, and I will give you rest" (Matthew 11:28). The other, reaching for a different sheet, reads, "In him"—in Christ—"we have redemption through his blood, the forgiveness of our trespasses, according to the riches of his grace, which he lavished upon us" (Ephesians 1:7, 8). He again summarizes the gospel: "Christ is your priest! His blood is your sacrifice! His altar is your confessional!"

A wave of sacred joy sweeps over the gathering. Then come expressions of praise and thanksgiving mingled with exclamations of wonderment:

"Praise God for His graciousness to us!"

"No more long pilgrimages!"

"I may come to Jesus just as I am, sinful and unholy, and He says, 'Your sins are forgiven. You are washed in My blood.' "

"Hallelujah!"

After a few moments of silence adorned with tears of joy, one of the missionaries speaks a quiet celebration of the gospel in prayer. With warm hugs and continued praise to God, the new believers slip into the night.[8]

1. Eduard Norden, *Die antike Kunstprosa*, vol. 2, 4th ed. (Berlin: Teubner, 1923), quoted in Markus Barth, *Ephesians 1–3*, Anchor Bible 34 (Garden City, NY: Doubleday, 1974), 77.

2. Eugene H. Peterson, *Practice Resurrection: A Conversation on Growing Up in Christ* (Grand Rapids, MI: Eerdmans, 2010), 54.

3. The teaching of Calvinistic predestination also uses Romans 8:28–30; 9:22, 23; 1 Timothy 1:9.

4. Philip Schaff, *The Creeds of the Evangelical Protestant Churches*, vol. 3 of *The Creeds of Christendom, With a History and Critical Notes*, 4th ed. (New York: Harper & Bros., 1919), 608, 609.

5. Ralph P. Martin, *Ephesians, Colossians, and Philemon*, Interpretation (Atlanta: John Knox, 1991), 91.

6. Peterson, *Practice Resurrection*, 61.

7. Peterson, 63.

8. I have imagined this scene based on Ellen G. White's account in *The Great Controversy* (Mountain View, CA: Pacific Press®, 1950), 73–75.

3

The Power of
the Exalted Jesus

Ephesians 1:15-23

As I approach the display case in the British Library, I already know the story behind what it holds. British explorer Robert Scott and his four companions reached the South Pole on January 17, 1912, only to discover that the Norwegians had beaten them to the pole. In a discouraged and ill-fated attempt to return to their supply base, all five perished. Scott and his last two companions died just eleven miles from the next supply depot. Eight long months passed before the discovery of the treasure I am about to see—Scott's journal of the expedition, dubbed by one British newspaper, "A great book, perhaps the greatest ever written."[1] There it is—the original journal of Robert Scott, softly lit and opened to his famous "Last Entry" with its poignant, penciled words: "For God's sake look after our people." What a valuable historical treasure!

It pales, though, in comparison with another journal entry. This one is from a much older document, hailing not from the twentieth century but the first. Like Scott's journal entry, it is written by one who senses that his end may be near. A unique record, it is a leaf from the prayer journal of the great early Christian missionary—the apostle

Paul. Today, we approach the display case and ponder his ancient words found in Ephesians 1:15–23.

False gods and goddesses

As with Scott's journal, we need to recall the backstory to appreciate this treasure's immense value. I wish we could stroll together down the streets of first-century Ephesus, watching merchants hawk their wares, listening to itinerant philosophers seeking to gather an audience, and following some of its citizens as they move through their day. If we could do so, we would experience the pervasive presence of religion in their lives. They believed that their existence was under the control of the gods—the divinized stars and planets—and was subject to the Fates.[2] It was unlikely that a person could escape the set, dark destiny prescribed by the specific pattern of stars and planets at one's birth. But one had to try.

As a result, worshiping the many gods and goddesses was a staple of first-century life, especially the worship of Artemis, the patron goddess of Ephesus, who was worshiped through sacrifices, chants and hymns, and public ceremonies and festivals, especially by following the the sacred statue of Atemis on winding, sacred route around Mount Pion. Worshiping the gods and goddesses in the privacy of one's home shrine. Attempting to worship the right god or goddess at the right moment in just the right way to avert the evil that perhaps was in store. This reality invaded every aspect of life. Books of magic (Acts 19), charms, amulets, talismans, thunderstones, and the like bear witness to the attempts of the ancient residents of Ephesus to influence their fate.

A famous ancient sports story illustrates all this. A wrestler from Ephesus, competing in the games in Olympia—the Olympics—meets with remarkable success. In match after match, he proves the victor. Until, during a match with a wrestler from Miletus, a referee spies something around his ankle. It turns out to be a small amulet inscribed with the "Ephesian letters," which were six magical, nonsense words that were etched on the cult statue of Artemis and were regarded as mysterious and powerful. As the story relates, the amulet is removed, and the wrestler from Ephesus, deprived of his magic, suffers defeats against his opponent from Miletus in three successive matches. The purpose of the story? To argue for the importance and power of magic, invoking words and names to influence the future.

It is to the people in this historical setting that Paul writes and prays for. He is concerned that the addressees will be drawn again into relying on a whole range of "names" and "powers." So he alerts them to how he prays for them. Having heard of their conversion and their "love toward all the saints" (verse 15), he describes his dedicated, continual prayers on their behalf (verse 16). He makes one main request for them: the Spirit (verse 17).[3] He has just affirmed that they received the Holy Spirit at their conversion (verses 13, 14). Here he prays that the Spirit might be active in bringing them specific spiritual insight about three grand spiritual realities for believers: (1) the hope of God's call (verse 18), (2) the riches of the glory of God's inheritance in the saints (verse 18), and (3) the exceeding greatness of His power exercised on behalf of believers (verse 19).

The hope

The first of these heartening realities—"the hope to which he has called you" (verse 18)—refers to God's call to the believers in the past (Ephesians 1:3–9, 11–13; 2:12), which resulted in their conversion, and to the grand Christian hope for the future (Ephesians 1:14; 4:4). Rather than succumbing to the doleful future assigned by the Fates, they are to look to the future God has designed for them. Paul prays for fresh insight from the Spirit that believers might understand a second great reality: "The riches of the glory of His inheritance in the saints" (Ephesians 1:18, NKJV). Based on Old Testament concepts (Deuteronomy 9:29; 32:9; Zechariah 2:12), Paul has already thought of the saints as God's inheritance, His treasure trove (Ephesians 1:11), and he returns to that thought here. He wishes them to know their value to God as it is a central element in their Christian identity. They not only possess God's inheritance (verses 14; Ephesians 3:6; cf. Ephesians 5:5) but also *are* God's inheritance![4]

Paul focuses most of his attention on the third magnificent spiritual reality that he prays the Spirit will activate in the lives of believers: "The immeasurable greatness of his power toward us who believe" (Ephesians 1:19). For Paul, the dynamic, effective power of the Holy Spirit in the lives of believers has its source in four important salvation-history events that have already occurred, each of which is something God the Father did for His Son, Jesus Christ. The Father (1) raised Jesus from the dead (verse 20), (2) "seated him at his right hand" (verses 20), (3) "put all things under his feet" (verse 22), and (4) "gave him as head over all things to the church" (verse 22).

Look at Jesus!

"Look at Jesus where He was—the poor, tortured, wounded body, slain by our sins, lying cold and still in Joseph's grave: then lift up your eyes and see Him where He is,—enthroned in the worship and wonder of heaven! Measure by that distance, by the sweep and lift of that almighty Arm, the strength of the forces engaged to your salvation, the might of the powers at work through the ages for the redemption of humanity."[5]

Name above all names

This prayer request of Paul's constitutes one of the most important descriptions of the exaltation of Jesus that we find in the New Testament. Paul wishes those addressees in Ephesus, tempted to acknowledge the power of other names, to understand that Jesus had been exalted by the Father, that His name is far more powerful and effective than any phonemes attached to any deity of choice worshiped in their city. Jesus is "seated" in the most important place—at the "right hand" of the Father. This coronation has occurred "in the heavenly places" (verse 20), where, by virtue of being exalted to the Father's throne, Jesus is now "far above all rule and authority and power and dominion" (verse 21).

Paul does not list every possible label for evil or spiritual powers or describe any hierarchy among these powers. He does seek to be comprehensive, making it clear that *all* supernatural powers are under the authority of the exalted Jesus. To make sure that his readers get the point that absolutely every supernatural power owes allegiance to the exalted Jesus, he adds a phrase that echoes the religious practice in Ephesus: "And above every name that is named" (verse 21). With those early believers, we are carried upward on the wings of Paul's prayer, invited to exult with them in the Resurrection exaltation-coronation of Jesus.

Paul wishes his readers to understand something more about the exaltation of Jesus to the throne of the cosmos: It is no temporary appointment. His domain is unlike the rule of the deities of Ephesus, which were effective for some limited segment of the calendar—an hour, a day, or a month. No! Christ's lordship is dynamic (moving with time) and not static (to be surpassed in time). It is for all time, unaffected by transitions from age to age. Christ's exaltation applies "not only in this age but also in the one to come" (verse 21).

In line with the Jewish understanding of two ages, which include the present age and "the one to come," Paul foresees a coming shift in the ages. He believes that "this age," marked as it is in our fallen world by the rule of the "prince of the power of the air, the spirit that is now at work in the sons of disobedience," dominating, subjugating, and corrupting humankind (Ephesians 2:1–3), will soon end. It will give way to "the age to come," in which Christ's rule, already inaugurated by His exaltation to the right hand of God, will be extended throughout the cosmos. That coming shift will not, says Paul, diminish in any

The exaltation of Jesus in the Psalms

Paul hears the exaltation of Jesus echoed in the Psalms.

Psalm 110 is one of the most often used Old Testament passages in all the New Testament, and Paul alludes to it here when he affirms that God seated Christ (which means "the anointed one," the anointed King) "at his right hand in the heavenly places" (Ephesians 1:20; cf. Acts 2:33–35; Colossians 3:1; Hebrews 1:3, 4, 13; 8:1; Revelation 5:1, 7; Romans 8:34). Compare Psalm 110:1, where "the LORD" says to the Messianic figure, "Sit at my right hand."

In describing that God "put all things under his feet" (Ephesians 1:22), Paul quotes Psalm 8:6 from the Greek Old Testament, the first direct quotation from the Old Testament in Ephesians. The thought that "all things," in the sense of "all rule and authority and power and dominion, and . . . every name that is named" (Ephesians 1:21), are subjugated to Christ is also expressed in Psalm 110: " 'Sit at my right hand, until I make your enemies your footstool.' . . . Rule in the midst of your enemies!" (verses 1, 2).

way the lordship of Jesus that has been celebrated and initiated at God's throne. In fact, the coming age will be marked by actualizing everywhere, including our errant planet, the lordship of Christ over all things, fulfilling the plan the Father laid "before the foundation of the world" (Ephesians 1:4).

Christ, you see, is not subject to eschatology (last-day events). He is the Subject of eschatology, the goal of God's grand, fullness-of-time strategy, the only time scheme that matters (verses 9, 10). To make sure that we have not missed the point that the rule of the exalted Christ over all things is for all time, Paul will soon declare God's purpose: "That in the coming ages he might show the immeasurable riches of his grace in kindness toward us in Christ Jesus" (Ephesians 2:7). In the present, at the heart of the cosmos, on the throne of God, sits Jesus. After the tumult of the end of time, when the smoke has cleared, there on the universal throne will be Jesus. For time immemorial, age upon endless age, every glimpse of that cosmic throne finds Jesus ruling all things for all time.

Paul does not describe the boundless authority and limitless time frame of Christ's rule as a mere detail of cosmological chronology or a snippet of heavenly trivia. He means for it to impact the present in the lives of believers who are constantly tempted to see various deities as ruling over this period of time or that. Such an understanding is embedded in the Roman calendar we employ today, which, for example, labels the fifth day of the week as Thursday, Thor's day, under the special rule and oversight of the god Thor (the Norse god of thunder, equivalent to the Roman god Jupiter). Every moment, every hour, every day, every month, every year, and every age, argues Paul, is Christ's. If you would spend those periods well, they must be invested in the service of the Ruler over all things and every period, the Lord Jesus Christ. Do not waste your Thursdays on Thor, Paul says. They belong to Jesus!

"The God of our Lord Jesus Christ . . . raised him from the dead and seated him at his right hand in the heavenly places, far above all rule and authority and power and dominion, and above every name that is named, not only in this age but also in the one to come" (Ephesians 1:17, 20, 21). This means that in this age and at this time, there is

- no brand name,
- no famous name,
- no political name,
- no powerful name,
- no Hollywood name,

- no rich name,
- no smart name,
- no media name,
- no entrepreneur's name,
- no preacher's name,
- no party name,
- no philanthropist's name,
- no academic degree's name,
- no classy, fashionable name,
- no boss's name,
- no tycoon's name,
- no multinational corporation's name,
- no sophisticated, literary name,
- no URL name,
- no god's or goddess's name,
- no family name,
- no mover and shaker's name,
- no mentor's name,
- no drink's name,
- no sports name,
- no social media name,
- no institution's name, and
- no church's name

that can make the difference in your life that this name can make: our Lord Jesus Christ.

---

1. *Daily Graphic*, November 6, 1913, 7.

2. The Fates were three mythical sisters, goddesses who appear in Greek and Roman mythology, and were regarded as together determining human destinies at the time of a

person's birth, especially the span of one's life.

3. As the passage should likely be understood. Some translations speak of "a spirit" instead of "the Spirit," believing that Paul refers to the believers' own attitude or disposition. However, it is difficult to imagine a human spirit "of revelation" because revelation comes through the Holy Spirit.

4. Alternatively, the phrase may be understood as a restatement of the first element of spiritual insight for which Paul asks: the future hope or inheritance that God provides to Christians.

5. George Gillanders Findlay, *The Epistle to the Ephesians* (New York: Ray Long & Richard R. Smith, 1931), 77, 78.

4

How God Rescues Us

Ephesians 2:1-10

Entering the city's university for the new term is tricky business for young, bright scholars. You have good reason to be cautious. A few years back, your parents became converts to the Way, to Christianity. Amazing stories, still often told, hark back to that time—stories about miracles and healing. Just the touch of an apron or handkerchief was enough to do it. Back then, members of the Way, followers of the Lord Jesus, were so successful in attracting converts that income to the great temple of Artemis plummeted. The whole tourism industry suffered as well. A huge riot broke out at the amphitheater, leading to a lot of sore throats for citizens who shouted for two hours: "Great is Artemis of the Ephesians!" This may not have been good public relations for the fledgling sect, but the point is this: Back then, Christianity was influential, the latest thing, a force to be reckoned with. To be a member of the Way had a certain cachet, clout, and standing.

Over the years, life has drifted back to "normal." Pilgrimages to the temple of Artemis have returned to their usual levels. Silver shrines of the goddess again sell at a fast clip. The monthlong spring festival honoring Artemis is again well attended. Her athletic contests, theatrical shows, musical concerts, and sumptuous banquets are as glorious and well subscribed as ever. All the best bands play their songs in her parades. The lyrics of the most popular tunes croon loyalty to her. The big companies sponsor her feasts and bask in their loyalty to her. If you are honest, you feel the tug of all of this. Being a member of the Way, a follower of the Lord Jesus, does not carry the influence it once did. It no longer opens doors; instead, it shuts them. To worship the Lord Jesus is to risk becoming a pariah—and an impoverished one at that.

It has been natural, then, to consider coping strategies and ways to soften the edges of your Christian identity. Would it really hurt to attend one of the feasts now and again and sip the libations? Perhaps your witness of Jesus might be better heard if you were not so odd and out of step with the culture around you. You have even been missing the Friday evening Bible study; the one held discreetly in a disciple's home, with guests entering through a back alley. You have heard, though, that a letter has come from Paul, the great apostle who preached Christianity here in the first place. Tychicus, a close associate of Paul's, has come to town, and he will share Paul's message, performing the letter rather than just reading it. It will be almost like hearing Paul himself! So, you tread warily down the back alley, your Christian identity needing a boost, and enter the house church.

Warm greetings in the name of the Lord Jesus. Hugs. Good food. Then, with the group gathered and hushed, Tychicus stands for the performance. You listen to these words: "You were dead in the trespasses and sins in which you once walked, following the course of this world, following the prince of the power of the air, the spirit that is now at work in the sons of disobedience—among whom we all once lived in the passions of our flesh, carrying out the desires of the body and the mind, and were by nature children of wrath, like the rest of mankind" (Ephesians 2:1–3).

How God Rescues Us

Plan A

We sit today with those challenged disciples of old, those Christian college students at Ephesus University. What do these words mean to us? What messages do they convey? In Ephesians 2:1–3, Paul describes plan A. Given our sinful world, it seems the default plan for our lives. It is Satan's plan. While still bearers of the image of God, we have come to understand that there is something deeply awry in us. Living the Christian life, then, is not just a matter of conquering a pesky, bad habit or overcoming whatever "trespasses and sins" (verse 1) are currently threatening. We do not just contend with sins but with *sin*. We are bent toward rebellion against God and toward self-destruction. Humans, by default, are caught in a pattern of self-destructive, sinful behavior, following the dictates of Satan (verse 2) and our innate, sinful desires. Believers once were "by nature children of wrath" (verse 3).

It is important to note that in offering this description, Paul employs a past tense: we "were by nature children of wrath" (verse 3). This does not mean that an inherent bent toward evil is no longer a reality for believers. Paul spends a considerable portion of his letter warning that sinful acts, rooted in a sinful nature, remain a threat for Christians (especially Ephesians 4:17–5:21). It does mean, though, that this "old self" needs no longer dominate the believer, who, through the power of Christ, can "put off" the "old self" and "put on the new self, created after the likeness of God in true righteousness and holiness" (Ephesians 4:22, 24). In this light, the description of plan A in Ephesians 2:1–3 invites searching questions: Is my life all too marked by the sins, passion, and dominance by Satan that Paul describes here? Is the past life of the believers in Ephesus my present?

Plan C

The good news is that plan A is not the only plan available to us. For you see, there is plan C—the Christ-shaped, Christ-determined,

Christ-created, and Christ-saturated life made possible by the mercy and grace of God. Plan C: "But God, being rich in mercy, because of the great love with which he loved us, even when we were dead in our trespasses, made us alive together with Christ—by grace you have been saved—and raised us up with him and seated us with him in the heavenly places in Christ Jesus, so that in the coming ages he might show the immeasurable riches of his grace in kindness toward us in Christ Jesus" (verses 4–7).

One writer describes the shift from plan A to plan C in the passage this way: "The grim, plodding, hopeless, long-syllabled announcement of human lostness—dead in trespasses and sins, children of wrath by nature—is shattered by a lightning bolt from heaven . . . [introducing] the greatest short statement in the history of human language: 'But God, because he is rich in mercy' (verse 4)."[1]

Paul drenches these verses in God's mercy, love, and grace. Before he describes any action God has taken, he identifies central elements of God's character—His mercy (Greek, *eleos*) and love (Greek, *agapē*)—as the origins of those gracious actions. In Paul's view, salvation is a deeply personal and relational initiative for God. Salvation is not a mechanical, legal process, offered by a distant judge with little personal interest in our case. This is a Father mounting a rescue of His beloved children (Ephesians 2:19; 3:14, 15; 4:6; 5:1). It is heart work with Him. He responds based on His character of mercy and love, which are directed very personally toward us. He cannot help Himself!

According to Ephesians 2:4–7, God has done three amazing things for us:

1. He "made us alive together with Christ." We participate in Christ's resurrection.
2. He "raised us up with him." We participate in Christ's ascension.
3. He "seated us with him in the heavenly places." We participate in Christ's exaltation and coronation.

What does it mean to experience co-resurrection, co-ascension, and co-exaltation with Christ?

To understand and apply this passage, we must remind ourselves of the relationship of the resurrected, ascended, and exalted Jesus to "the powers." Paul's hearers—and all humankind—once served "the rulers and authorities in the heavenly places" (Ephesians 3:10), worshiping and paying obeisance to various astral powers and having only a destructive pattern of life ("dead in the trespasses and sins," Ephesians 2:1) to show for it. Paul does not deny the existence of these evil and demonic powers nor their ability to dominate human life. However—and it is a big "however"—in the resurrection, ascension, and exaltation of Jesus, they have, in God's mercy-driven and grace-filled plan, been thoroughly superseded. Their hold on human existence has been made obsolete. In these salvation-history events centered in the Messiah, the cosmos has shifted. Reality has changed.

There are some Bible passages that break open, spilling their meaning at your feet, astonishing with their fully disclosed impact. Others offer a suggestive flash of insight but seem to hide much of their full meaning, wrapping it in mystery and wonder, evoking worship as much for what they withhold as what they reveal. Ephesians 2:4–7 is, for me, of this latter type. What does it really mean to be co-resurrected, co-ascended, and co-exalted with Christ?

Is it *liturgical*? Is it an invitation to participate in heaven's worship service? Is this the letter form of the invitation issued to John in Revelation 4:1?[2] With a door flung open in heaven, there comes the summons, "Come up here!" Join in the worship service of praise going on before the throne!

Is it *representative*? Christ, in experiencing resurrection, ascension, and exaltation, represents believers. We experience these cosmic acts through Him as our Representative.

Is it *participatory*? Because of our solidarity with Christ, do we somehow participate in His resurrection, ascension, and exaltation?

Is it *relational*? When my older brother Bill, leading the trumpet trio in playing "Bugler's Holiday" in the Walla Walla College talent show, wins the grand prize, my stock goes up. Why? Because he is my brother. What is good for him is great for me!

Is it (scare quotes) *"astrological"*? The foundational principle of astrology is this: when something important happens in the heavens, it triggers a parallel event on Earth. In a true reflection of that principle, do Christ's resurrection, ascension, and exaltation up there trigger spiritual resurrection, ascension, and exaltation for us down here?

Is this a case of *patterning* or *trajectory*? Christ, in His resurrection, ascension, and exaltation, scribes an arc across the cosmos—one punctuated by these cosmos-shifting events, a pattern or trajectory that we are now empowered to retrace as His disciples and His followers.

Is it *illustrative*? Ephesians 1:19–23, which occurs just before our passage, is an important description of the exaltation of Jesus. Paul highlights the power of God illustrated in the resurrection and exaltation of Jesus "far above all rule and authority and power and dominion and above every name that is named, not only in this age but also in the one to come. And he put all things under his feet" (verses 21, 22). Stunningly, the divine power of God exercised in Christ's resurrection and His exaltation to the unbounded domain and absolute authority illustrate the power available to believers. That power is the source of the resurrection, ascension, and exaltation of believers!

I may be exhausting you in my attempt to explore Paul's meaning. But I am in no way exhausting the meaning of Paul's implied story: once the enemies of God, now through His grace-driven initiative in Christ, we stand co-resurrected, co-ascended, and co-exalted with Jesus.

Raised up to heavenly places

Allow me to illustrate a cluster of meanings for this language:

representative, participatory, and *relational*. Imagine this scenario: You were really special to each other way back in the eighth grade. Best friends forever! You have not seen your friend in years. You do not have a clue where she lives or what he is doing with his life. Your cell phone vibrates and displays an unfamiliar number from a distant state. You answer, and lo and behold, it is that long-lost best friend calling. There is some chitchat, a little catching up, and then comes this line: "I need to tell you a story." So, the story spills out. Your once BFF has just won that distant state's lottery—a new car, a new house, and $1 million a year for life. The story drones on for a while. You try to connect to it, to listen. You wonder why you need to hear this story. Is your once best friend just gloating? Did your friend call to rub it in, to bask in success at your expense?

Then, the story over, your old friend says, "You are probably wondering why I called." (Well, yes!) "Here's the thing: when I signed up for that lottery ticket, it had spaces for two names." Suddenly, the story becomes more interesting; you are listening more intently. "I wrote my name on the line, and I was going to leave it at that. Then your face came clearly to mind. I thought of you, my first best friend. On a whim, I wrote your name on that line. Half the loot is yours! What is your current address?"

Lotteries that someone else wins are not all that interesting. But when the loot is yours, it is different. You really have won this lottery. This story—this story of Jesus—is not just long ago, far away, and disconnected from your own. You are resurrected with Christ. You are raised with Him. You are exalted with Him. You are royal because He is royal. There is a place on His throne with your name inscribed on it! This is who you really are. This is your identity right now and your eternal destiny. By God's merciful design, you are so tight with the Lord Jesus Christ that His story is your story. We are not mere spectators to these cosmos-shifting, reality-changing events. Believers are so personally and intimately involved that Paul can say we have been co-resurrected, co-ascended, and co-exalted with the Messiah, Jesus Christ (Ephesians 2:4–6).

That being the case, a whole new array of possibilities opens before us. We have the right to turn from a demon-dominated existence to a God-crafted life (verse 7; cf. verses 8–10). "Those who are united to Christ have no need to pay their respects to those forces over which he has vindicated his preeminence."[3] Paul will acknowledge in the last half of the letter (especially Ephesians 6:10–20) that this is no simple transition for us. The dominance of the powers and the corresponding negative pattern of life have real staying power. So we must constantly rehearse, celebrate, and relive the story of Christ's resurrection, ascension, and exaltation-coronation and our part in them, just as Paul is modeling in Ephesians 2:4–7. To do so is surely close to the heart of Christian faith, identity, and discipleship. We should read these verses regularly in the company of the biblical records of the following events in Christ's life:

- Christ's resurrection (Matthew 28; Mark 16; Luke 24; John 20; 1 Corinthians 15)
- Christ's ascension (Mark 16:19; Luke 24:50–53; Acts 1:6–11)
- Christ's coronation (Acts 2:33–36; Revelation 4; 5)

We must hold in our consciousness plan C—the Christ-shaped, Christ-determined, Christ-created, and Christ-saturated life made possible by the mercy and grace of God: "But God, being rich in mercy, because of the great love with which he loved us, even when we were dead in our trespasses, made us alive together with Christ—by grace you have been saved—and raised us up with him and seated us with him in the heavenly places in Christ Jesus, so that in the coming ages he might show the immeasurable riches of his grace in kindness toward us in Christ Jesus" (Ephesians 2:4–7).

1. S. M. Baugh, *Ephesians*, Evangelical Exegetical Commentary (Bellingham, WA: Lexham, 2016), 141, 153.

2. See the introduction to chapter 2.

3. F. F. Bruce, *The Epistles to the Colossians, to Philemon, and to the Ephesians*, New International Commentary on the New Testament (Grand Rapids, MI: Eerdmans, 1984), 102.

5

Horizontal Atonement:
The Cross and the Church

Ephesians 2:11-22

Peter Strelzyk hatched the idea in March 1978. A balloon! They would escape East Germany, with its constant surveillance and oppression, in a balloon. His friend, Günter Wetzel, posed the obvious question: "Great, and where do we find a balloon?" Neither had any aeronautical experience. Günter was a bricklayer and truck driver; Peter, a foreman in a plastics factory. So, they began to read everything they could find about hot-air balloons. They quickly discovered that they would need a huge balloon to transport themselves and their families—a total of four adults, one teenager, and three smaller children—a balloon with a volume of seventy thousand cubic feet, requiring nearly nine thousand square feet of material.

They bought a huge supply of cotton fabric in a larger town some thirty miles away. "We are members of a camping club," they explained. Working on a forty-year-old foot-pedal sewing machine, they fashioned the balloon in just two weeks. They constructed a small platform with a clothesline guardrail to serve as a gondola. They also created a burner and blower, all from their meager resources. However, several clandestine tests revealed that the cotton cloth was too porous. So they destroyed the evidence, burning eight hundred yards of cotton cloth in the home furnace for several weeks.

Undaunted, they drove a hundred miles to Leipzig and bought taffeta material, explaining they were from a sailing club. They attached an electric motor to the sewing machine, and within a week, they had a new balloon. Now, though, they discovered that the burner was too weak to do the job. And it was getting too late in the year and too cold to make a flight. The Wetzel family gave up on the scheme.

July 3, 1979, finally brought the right weather and wind conditions. On July 4, at 1:30 A.M., the Strelzyk family inflated the balloon and lifted off. They soared quickly to an altitude of sixty-six hundred feet. The wind was blowing them toward West Germany at a good clip, twenty miles per hour. Then they entered a cloud. Vapor condensed onto the material, making it heavier and heavier. The balloon came down quickly. When they climbed out, they found themselves a scant two hundred yards from the border and freedom. July 4 was not to be Independence Day for the Strelzyks.[1]

The great wall basher

I can think of few good reasons for mourning the destruction of the Berlin Wall and the razing of the Iron Curtain. In fact, I can identify only one: I miss those inspiring stories of incredibly courageous people seeking freedom. Shortly after the wall came down, a nephew gave me a gift in a little maroon velvet pouch. Opening it, I found some nondescript pieces of concrete and a "Declaration of Authenticity and Origin" that read: "You have just purchased a piece of history; a fragment of the Berlin Wall. We have verified the authenticity and origin of this rock after careful investigation. The Berlin Wall, which was constructed during the height of the Cold War, has remained intact for nearly 28 years. In November 1989, portions of the Berlin Wall, a part of which you now own, was torn down to create free passage to the West. Enjoy and treasure your fragment of freedom." I have indeed treasured my "fragment of freedom" and now, decades later, wonder at the fact that the Berlin Wall has now been demolished for longer than it stood.

In Ephesians 2:11–22, Paul portrays Christ as the great wall basher. The passage is arguably the most important one in the Bible on the theme of race relations. While the setting Paul addresses in these verses—the alienation of Jews and Gentiles—may seem a distant one for many of us, the passage divulges broad principles about salvation history and the relationships among people groups in it that remain transformative for us today. In this passage, the Holy Spirit brings us a challenging agenda for spiritual growth. The Spirit calls us to identify our own walls, our own alienation from others, and then to experience for ourselves—in the company of those we have despised—the reconciling work of Christ, centered in the Cross. The purpose of this chapter is to guide you in the challenging work of understanding and applying this valuable passage.

Ephesians 2:11–22 is a big-picture passage offering a sweeping sketch of the plan of salvation in three sections:

1. Why the reconciling work of Christ was necessary (verses 11, 12)
2. The wall-bashing and reconciling work of Christ (verses 13–18)
3. Celebrating the reconciling work of Christ (verses 19–22)

It is important to note the way Paul begins. He has just portrayed the dramatic transformation his addressees have experienced from Satan-dominated subservience to their base passions (verses 1–3) to becoming subjects of God's grace, experiencing spiritual resurrection (verses 4–10), and being enthroned "in the heavenly places in Christ Jesus" (verse 6). Given the wonders of their new existence, one might think that it would be best to forget their jaded past. Paul, though, calls them to remember that past, especially one aspect of it: their former hatred toward and alienation from Jews. Paul knows that sin—not just sins but *sin*, how we humans are all too naturally bent away from God and righteousness and toward selfishness—still threatens Christians. So Paul asks them to carefully differentiate their former attitudes, prejudices, and mindset from the work of Christ in their midst.

Paul means for the work of Christ to be compellingly active among believers. Christ, on the cross, brings the far near, makes peace, destroys what divides, creates a whole new way of being human, reconciles Jews and Gentiles in His body—the church—and slays the hostility between Jews and Gentiles (verses 13–16). Having done all of that, He trumpets the good news of His accomplishments both to hopeless Gentiles ("to you who were far off") and to smug Jews ("to those who were near," verse 17). He then escorts both into the throne room of God, introducing them to His Father, giving both groups shared "access in one Spirit to the Father" (verse 18).

We must be able to differentiate the principles and strategies that dominated our demon-determined past from the principles and strategies exercised by Christ, which He intends to be active in our Christ-shaped present and future. Only then will we be able to test and judge our reactions in any moment and situation. Through the influence of the Spirit, we may then choose life and choose to follow the pattern set forth by Christ. We may once again turn from the icy hand of selfishness, sin, separation, and alienation and grasp the life-giving, peacemaking hand of Jesus.

Self-examination

Paul's powerful sketch of the reconciling work of Christ in verses 13–18 offers a set of questions for the important work of self-examination, inviting us to weigh the impact of our influence and perceive our dividing walls. These are serious, searching questions that we must ask in a Spirit-inspired attitude of humility and repentance:

- *Verse 13*: Am I, in company with Christ, bringing the far near, or am I keeping people who are not like me at a distance?
- *Verse 14*: Am I, in company with Christ, fostering peace between races, or am I ramping up the violence and hostility?
- *Verse 15*: Am I, in company with Christ, making peace, or am I declaring war?
- *Verses 14, 15*: Am I, in company with Christ, breaking down what divides people groups, or am I building up the walls between them?
- *Verse 16*: Am I, in company with Christ, building on the work of peacemaking by advancing the reconciliation of the races, especially within the church but also in society at large, or am I seeking to divide and separate?
- *Verses 17, 18*: Am I, in company with Christ, preaching peace and fostering shared access by all, or am I preaching hatred and limiting access for some?

I have come to especially treasure verse 18: "For through him [the crucified Christ by whose death the hostility between Jew and Gentile has been slain (verses 13–16), and the risen Christ who preaches to both Jew and Gentile the peace He won on Calvary (verse 17)] we both [Jews and Gentiles] have access in one Spirit to the Father." Here Paul brings together the *vertical* atonement of Christ (the forgiveness of our sins, the mending of our relationship with God, our ability to stand blameless in God's presence, and the individual application of God's grace) with the *horizontal* atonement wrought by Christ (the shared status with those we once demeaned, the mended community between sworn enemies, the joint participation in God's initiative to create a new kind of reconciled humanity, and the communal application of God's grace in calling forth the church).

Given the context, especially the mention of the destruction of "the middle wall of separation" (verse 14, NKJV) and the temple imagery (verses 19–22), Paul seems to be thinking of "access" (Greek, *prosagōgē*; verse 18) in relation to the temple and the desire for access to worship God. "Access" implies more than being in someone's presence. Ancient author Xenophon tells of Sacas, the cupbearer, whose job it was to "introduce" (*prosagō*) those who wished to conduct business with Astyages, king of the Medes. Xenophon also describes how Cyrus expected anyone wishing for "access" (*prosagōgē*) to him to request it through his friends, who could grant entrance into the royal presence, along with the privilege of making requests of the king.[2] Such a background suggests the image of Christ as "the 'bringer' of the suppliant into God's presence."[3] Christ ushers us into the presence of God, where we are invited to make our requests to Him and do business with the King. Paul reminds us that when we enter to lay our business before the King, we discover that He is our Father.

We make another important discovery as well. We come, grace blessed and awed, into the presence of the King, assuming this access to be our exclusive right. However, in our peripheral vision, we detect the presence of another there in God's presence as well. The Jew finds there the one once hated, the Gentile; the Gentile finds the one once despised, the Jew. To claim, exercise, and enjoy the grand Christian blessing of Christ-won and Spirit-actuated access to the Father, it must be shared with those we once despised! Without the sharing, the blessing evaporates. To be active in our experience, we must share both forgiveness and access.

Having explored the necessity of Christ's work of reconciliation (verses 11, 12) and the nature of that work (verses 13–18), Paul now celebrates the reconciling work of Christ and the wondrous composition of the church out of Jews and Gentiles. To accent the solidarity of Jews and Gentiles in the church, he uses a series of metaphors that feed into each other—ones drawn from the content domains of immigration status ("no longer strangers and aliens, . . . you are fellow citizens with the saints," verse 19), family ("members of the household of God," verse 19), and architecture (the building of a temple, verses 20–22). In his culminating metaphor of inclusion, that of building a temple, he turns from his earlier language of demolition (verses 14–16) to that of construction, providing a creative and powerful image. Gentiles were excluded from the most sacred areas of the Jerusalem temple by a wall on which was posted the warning, "No foreigner may enter within the barrier and enclosure around the temple. Anyone caught doing so will have himself to blame for his ensuing death."[4] Paul announces that Christ, on the cross, destroys all such barriers (verses 14–16). Now Gentiles are included, not just as worshipers within a temple but as integral building materials of it. With Jewish believers, they "are being built together into a dwelling place for God by the Spirit" (verse 22).

Flee the barriers

In Ephesians 2:11–22, Paul, a Jew, is directly addressing Christian believers who are Gentiles, proclaiming their complete inclusion in the cause of God, in the church, and in God's plans for the world's future. Before you close your Bible, would you do something? Take a few prayerful moments, and identify that race or people group from which you feel most alienated, the one that gives rise in your heart to urges for separation and even condemnation. Visualizing members of that group whom you know, read this passage to them, substituting your own description of that group for Paul's description of Gentiles in verse 11. Having read the passage in that way, ask God's Spirit to help you rise up and live out this most powerful scriptural word on race relations.

After their failure, the Strelzyks, rejoined by the Wetzels, constructed one of the largest hot-air balloons ever made in Europe: over 141,000 cubic feet in capacity, 66 feet in diameter, and 82 feet high. The harrowing flight occurred on September 16, 1979. Making a hard landing, they sheltered in a barn. Inside, they saw a wagon inscribed with the farmer's name, something unheard of in the East. They knew they were free.[5]

Oh, that we might be half so determined to flee the barriers in our lives! Where will we find the lift to rise above our obsolete walls? "For he himself is our peace, who has made us both one and has broken down in his flesh the dividing wall of hostility" (Ephesians 2:14).

---

1. John Dornberg, "The Freedom Balloon," *Popular Mechanics*, February 1980, 100–102, 146–148.

2. Xenophon, *Cyropaedia* 1.3.8; 7.5.45, cited in David J. Williams, *Paul's Metaphors: Their Context and Character* (Peabody, MA: Hendrickson, 1999), 205.

3. Williams, 196, 205n38.

4. Walter C. Kaiser Jr., *The Promise-Plan of God: A Biblical Theology of the Old and New Testaments* (Grand Rapids, MI: Zondervan, 2008), 294.

5. Dornberg, "The Freedom Balloon," 148, 150; Jürgen Petschull, "The Great Balloon Escape," *Reader's Digest*, March 1980, 106–113.

6

The Mystery of the Gospel

Ephesians 3:1-21

His career starts with all the usual markers and trappings of success. He comes from a wealthy, highly privileged family. Having excelled in his early schooling, he is sent to an elite international institution. As a law student, he earns a stellar reputation as a scholar and attracts the loyalty of powerful mentors.

At the outset, his career follows suit. He serves ably, quickly moving up through the ranks. He marries well. In an amazingly short time, he has it all: an excellent salary; a happy, supportive family; a beautiful house; growing respect; and hopes for a rosy future. Soon, his name is being suggested for openings on important boards. When a pressing, high-profile, and challenging leadership opportunity presents itself, he steps into it with great energy, gaining applause for his strong leadership.

To this point, he would have been the poster boy for that common career advice, "Follow your passion!" Then the whole wondrous scenario comes unglued on a business trip connected to that latest leadership role. It is not due to some moral failing on his part—reports of drug use or a seamy extramarital affair. It happens en route to Damascus. In a blinding, life-altering vision, he meets Jesus.[1]

Paul, the mentor

In the wake of that moment, Saul of Tarsus loses everything that he had so painstakingly accumulated. Leaving behind his own passion, he adopts instead the passion of the risen, exalted Jesus. Much later, at an advanced point in his new and unexpected career, he reflects on his life journey. He admits that after the Damascus road experience, he "suffered the loss of all things" (Philippians 3:8). He asserts that he has long since cleared the balance sheet of his life, writing off all that went before as a total loss (verse 7). Looking back on decades of fulfillment in serving Christ, he has a label for all that went before: "rubbish," garbage (verse 8).

Now, in Ephesians 3, Paul again reflects on God's leading in his life. He begins the chapter by introducing a fresh prayer for his hearers (verse 1). Interrupting himself, he offers autobiographical reflections in verses 2–13 about his role in understanding and proclaiming "the mystery of Christ" (verse 4) before returning to his prayer, now shaped by the new sense of God's intervention in his life (verses 14–21).

Sharing mature reflections on his fascinating life and long career, the apostle Paul—arguably the greatest Christian missionary and leader of all time—steps forward to mentor you. As we review Paul's reflections on his own life (verses 1–13) and his prayer inspired by them (verses 14–21), we have the privilege of hearing his best career advice. He asserts that the world of résumés and interviews can deceive you. In that world, you must amplify your strengths and downplay or dismiss your weaknesses. For Paul, there is a wholly different perspective from which to examine and consider your life and career—one that he puts on full display in Ephesians 3. Paul's autobiographical sketch serves as an "anti-résumé." It is the usual résumé turned upside down, the well-polished curriculum vitae deconstructed. What powerful, inverted insights does he offer? What does true success look like? What are the most important principles for living a life of significance?

True success

Appearances can, indeed, be deceiving. True success does not always look very successful (verses 1, 13). Paul starts this mentoring session by touting a startling entry on his résumé—he is a prisoner (verse 1). In the honor-shame culture of which he is a part, this is no minor entry. To be a prisoner is a premier way to lose face. Being arrested and incarcerated is a sure way to destroy a solid career and a good reputation. He is concerned that his hearers will misinterpret the staggering fact of his imprisonment (verse 13), so he spends much of the chapter reframing his identity as a prisoner and helping them understand that true success often comes in disguise. He argues, "My being a prisoner is part of God's plan for my life and yours, part of our shared success story. In this upside-down résumé, composed by God's gracious intervention in my life, He has placed me right where He wishes me to be—in jail!"

Do not just tune in to your passion. Listen for God's call (verses 1–6). Had Paul continued to chase his passion, he would have missed God's revelation to him of "the mystery of Christ" (verse 4) and his calling to communicate that mystery to the Gentiles (verses 1, 2, 8). Meeting Jesus put Paul on a different path, allowing him to see that his passion moved against God's broader, richer plan for his life. Instead of a dead-end career, Paul's passions and gifts have been swallowed up in the grand project of proclaiming that God loves everyone and seeks the redemption of all.

Three Stanford University researchers recently argued against the common advice offered in commencement addresses: "Follow your passion!" Testing the belief systems that lead to success or failure, the researchers explored whether chasing one's own self-identified passion indicates success. Chronicling the behaviors of 470 participants, they concluded that following the common mantra could harm the chances for success in two ways: (1) by implying that the pathway to success will be quick and easy when the true path to success requires experimentation and failure, and (2) by narrowing one's focus too much when success requires multiple interests and the ability to make connections among them as the seedbed of innovation.[2] The researchers concluded, "Urging people to find their passion may lead them to put all their eggs in one basket but then to drop that basket when it becomes difficult to carry."[3]

Paul bears witness that releasing one's own passion and opening oneself to the broad purposes of God is a key to true success. While embracing our interests and passions, we must listen for God's call.

True success is all about getting caught up in God's grand plan. God is calling you into His great project—to unify all things in Christ (verses 1–6; cf. Ephesians 1:9, 10). In spite of being a prisoner, Paul is exuberant about the privilege he has had of playing a strategic role in God's great, end-all plan to unite everything in Christ. He can hardly believe that God tapped him on the shoulder (verse 2), shared His vision for the cosmos with him (verses 3–6), and tasked him with managing an essential part of the plan (verses 2, 7–10). While there are many ways to participate in that great project, God will never call you into a career that damages His ultimate plans for the cosmos. Like Paul, He is recruiting you to advance His goals. Seeking only your own honor and wealth pays limited dividends. In the end, you will need greater satisfaction and fulfillment than such a restricted scope of endeavor can offer.

The best opportunities are not earned based on your merit. They are gifts of God's grace (verses 7, 8). Paul lists another strange entry in this upside-down curriculum vitae: he claims to be "the very least of all the saints" (verse 8). He describes himself this way because he once persecuted Christian believers (Acts 8:1–3; 9:1, 2; 22:5, 6; 26:9–11; cf. 1 Timothy 1:15, where he labels himself "the foremost" of sinners). Despite that anguishing fact, he experienced "the gift of God's grace" (Ephesians 3:7) in the form of the commission to be the apostle to the Gentiles. The broader lesson is clear: true success for us all is marked by thanksgiving to God for His grace, not by hubris.

Ephesians

The scope of God's plan for you is vast. He imagines you engaged in cosmic leadership (verse 10). A good mentor will help you envision broader possibilities for your life. The best Mentor of all, reminds Paul, has cosmic-scale ambitions for you. As a member of the church, God intends to use you to reveal His multifaceted wisdom "to the rulers and authorities in the heavenly places" (verse 10; see the discussion of this verse in chapter 14). By valuing those who are different from you, you advance God's great showcase, which is the cross-cultural, multilingual community of the church (Revelation 14:6, 7). You contribute to God's grand plan to unify everything in Christ (Ephesians 1:9, 10) and help put the evil powers on notice that their rule is coming to an end. Note well: These amazing plans God has for you are not newly imagined; they are age-old ones! He has had them in place "for ages" (Ephesians 3:9; cf. Ephesians 3:11; 1:4).

Do not work for a boss. Join the family business. Work for your Father (Ephesians 3:14). Paul is in a Roman prison under the thumb of Emperor Nero himself. Yet Paul pays no obeisance to him. Instead, he writes, "I bow my knees before the Father" (verse 14). It is not Nero who is his jailer. He well remembers that it is another who captured him—ambushed him—long ago on the road to Damascus. Reflecting on that moment, he writes, "I press on to take hold of that for which Christ Jesus took hold of me" (Philippians 3:12, NIV). Ever since Christ apprehended him, Paul has lived his life under Christ's authority. He is not the prisoner of Nero. He is "a prisoner of Christ Jesus on behalf of you Gentiles" (Ephesians 3:1).

Be sure to choose a powerful Mentor who will provide you with everything you need (verses 14–19). When shopping for mentors who can foster success in their careers, people often look for a "big name" in their chosen field, perhaps the founder of an important company. As Paul returns to his prayer, he imagines for his hearers an amazing relationship with the biggest name of all: "The Father, from whom every family in heaven and on earth is named" (verses 14, 15). Every family and every business trace their origins to the One Paul imagines serving as your Mentor. He is the Founder of everything!

Great mentors share liberally with their mentees. They open fresh opportunities out of their resources: capital, networks of relationships, experience, and know-how. Paul prays that the Father will do so for believers—for you—drawing on His limitless resources "according to the riches of his glory" (verse 16).

The Father-Mentor

Ultimate satisfaction will not be found in accomplishments, projects, and to-do lists, however rewarding and necessary such things may be. Ultimate satisfaction comes through the ultimate relationship, your relationship with God (verses 14–19).

The most important resource any mentor can provide is a caring relationship. It is just here that Paul's prayer awes us in its sketch of the relationship he imagines between you and your Mentor. The Father-Mentor does not focus on job skills but on the heart, building your courage by affirming His confidence in you and His love for you (verses 17–19).

Landscape photographer Ansel Adams was mentored by his father, who "tenderly kept alive and glowing" an "internal spark."[4] As a result of your relationship with your Father, Paul imagines much more than fanning a little spark. He imagines that you will be "strengthened with power through his Spirit in your inner being" (verse 16). He envisions you being "rooted and grounded in love" (verse 17), growing in the firm conviction that God loves you. He expects you to experience the fathomless dimensions of "the love of Christ that surpasses knowledge" (verse 19).

The time commitment your Mentor makes to you is perhaps the most stunning feature of the relationship Paul anticipates. Paul does not think of just a half hour here or a lunch appointment there. Instead, he prays "that Christ may dwell in your hearts through faith" (verse 17). He prays that the Father, the Son, and the Spirit will share life with you so completely that you will be "filled with all the fullness of God" (verse 19).

God's plans for you—and what He will do through you, even if you are oblivious to it—will outstrip your ability to imagine and grasp His purposes in your life (verses 20, 21). Only in the ages of eternity will you be able to look back with head-shaking clarity and understand the full impact of a life dedicated to the grand purposes of God. If you hunger for true success, for a life of real meaning that fulfills a valuable purpose, take seriously Paul's countercultural, upside-down advice in Ephesians 3. From the perspectives of both time and eternity, you will be powerfully grateful that you did.

---

1. This modernized sketch of the early life of Saul of Tarsus reflects disputed suggestions about his life, especially that he was once married. For discussion and bibliography, see Raymond F. Collins, *Accompanied by a Believing Wife: Ministry and Celibacy in the Earliest Christian Communities* (Collegeville, MN: Liturgical Press, 2013), 123–138.

2. See Abigail Hess, "Stanford Researchers: 'Follow Your Passion' Advice Could Make You Less Successful," CNBC Make It, June 22, 2018, https://www.cnbc.com/2018/06/22/stanford-researchers-following-your-passion-makes-you-less-successful.html; Paul A. O'Keefe, Carol S. Dweck, and Gregory M. Walton, "Implicit Theories of Interest: Finding Your Passion or Developing It?," *Psychological Science* 29, no. 10 (October 2018): 1653–1664, https://doi.org/10.1177/0956797618780643.

3. O'Keefe, Dweck, and Walton, 1653.

4. Ansel Adams and Mary Street Alinder, *Ansel Adams: An Autobiography* (Boston: Little, Brown, 1985), 21.

7

The Unified Body of Christ

Ephesians 4:1-16

Our family once moved into a home named School House in the picturesque Peak District village of Cressbrook, near Buxton, in England. We transferred our few suitcases and moving crates into the ancient home. It had walls a couple of feet thick and five mismatched levels, but it was a godsend for us. It was comfortable, nicely furnished, and included books and knick-knacks. We settled in and soon discovered that our home was more than a large, one at the end of a long row of terrace houses; we were moving into a village with its own culture, history, interesting people to meet, and stories to be told. Moving into a house might take a few days. Moving into a village takes much longer. It is a slow process of long walks around the dale, chance encounters on the lane, playdates, visiting the neighbors, and participating in public events.

In Ephesians 1–3, Paul speaks to people who have experienced a dramatic move to a new location. Having once inhabited the land of death, trespasses, and sins (Ephesians 2:1), they now live in a new place in Christ (verses 4–10) and have been adopted into the family of God (verse 19). Now, though, comes the extended, more complex work of moving into the Christian village, signaled by a significant change of tone between chapters

3 and 4. Up to this point, Paul has offered "an exuberant exploration of who God is and the way he works." He has been preaching! Using "bold, urgent, excited, extravagant exuberance," Paul has described the location to which the believers have moved, now being "in Christ" and in the church. Now he adopts a "quieter, more conversational tone," one indicated by his introduction, "I therefore, a prisoner for the Lord, urge you to walk in a manner worthy of the calling to which you have been called" (Ephesians 4:1). He encourages believers to move into the Christ-shaped village. He draws them into detailed, thoughtful, and intimate conversation about what it means to be "in Christ."[1]

The Christian village

Early on our first Christmas morning in Cressbrook, we experienced a long-standing tradition. The Cressbrook Band showed up in full uniform and began playing a bright Christmas tune. Their brief performance of holiday favorites was followed by a time of fellowship, standing out in the lane with the band members. This pleasant Christmas surprise was a call to community, and Paul begins our passage with the same approach. Drawing on the theme at the heart of his letter, he urges believers to be "eager to maintain the unity of the Spirit in the bond of peace" (verse 3).

Then comes the music. The Christian village, too, has its favorite tunes. Paul now sings one of them; its hymnic lines affirm his exhortation and celebrate the unity of the church: "There is *one* body and *one* Spirit—just as you were called to the *one* hope that belongs to your call—*one* Lord, *one* faith, *one* baptism, *one* God and Father of all, who is over all and through all and in all" (verses 4–6; emphasis added). In the hymn, we celebrate the unity of the church as the fellowship created by Christ on the cross. This unity is not our work but God's. Irrespective of how well we may actualize it, our unity in these seven "ones" is a divinely crafted reality. We are one because God has made us one.

The Unified Body of Christ

When you move into a new village, it is important to become acquainted with who runs the place. Who is the mayor? Who are the members of the town council? Who is in charge of garbage collection? Who is the mail carrier? Paul spends most of our passage, verses 7–16, exploring how the Christian village—the church—is staffed. His introduction is exceptionally important, revealing the unique staffing pattern of the Christian village: "But grace was given to each one of us according to the measure of Christ's gift" (verse 7).

The church, as the new, unified humanity created by Christ on the cross (Ephesians 2:14, 15), does not depend on a few members to do its work. It is staffed by all. As believers, we hold many things in common, including the seven "ones" Paul has just celebrated in song. However, every church member is given a special "grace" of ministry "according to the measure of Christ's gift" (Ephesians 4:7), a phrase identifying the exalted Christ as the One who gives this grace. So Paul begins the segment (verses 1–16) with the idea that every citizen plays a vital role in running the Christian village (verse 7). He ends on the same note, expressing the point as part of the body metaphor. The church should function as the body of Christ, with "each part . . . working properly," helping the body to "grow so that it builds itself up in love" (verse 16). God is not interested in His village being dominated by a few but for all to be active, invested, and engaged.

Spiritual gifts

The topic of spiritual gifts is also addressed in several other places in the New Testament: Romans 12:3–8; 1 Corinthians 12; 14; and 1 Peter 4:7–11. These passages make the point that is so important to Paul here: all church members are equipped to participate in ministry. The passages also provide lists of these gifts that are given. Each list offers a different, though overlapping, set of gifts, which suggests that none of the lists is comprehensive. The gifts they disclose fall into two broad categories: "ministry in word" and "ministry in deed" (e.g., miracles, healing, administration, and showing mercy).[2] In this last half of Ephesians, Paul will allude to the ministries of deed mentioned in these other lists of spiritual gifts. For example, Paul could be referring to the gift of giving (Romans 12:8) in Ephesians 4:28 ("So that he may have something to share with anyone in need") and the gift of mercy or compassion (Romans 12:8) in Ephesians 4:32 ("Be kind to one another, tenderhearted, forgiving one another, as God in Christ forgave you").[3]

Paul will now focus on "ministry in word" and "ministers of the word." He begins by sharing a snippet from Psalm 68, which divulges as large and foundational a story as the quote is brief: "When he ascended on high he led a host of captives, and he gave gifts to men" (Ephesians 4:8, quoting Psalm 68:18). The "he" in the quote is Yahweh, who as the Divine Warrior has stepped onto the battlefield of history in defense of His people. Having won a great victory, He ascends the "mount" to His capital city (Psalm 68:16), leading a host of those He has taken captive (verse 18). Having arrived in His capital, He does what conquering generals do at such a moment: He gives gifts from the captured booty to those who have helped Him win the victory.[4]

For Paul, Jesus is the One who ascends to the heights of heaven. Exalted at the right hand of the Father, He distributes gifts to His people. This is a retelling of the story of Pentecost, when the exalted Jesus pours out the Holy Spirit as a sign of His coronation, and it is a story about the generosity of Jesus, who is portrayed as a conquering general rewarding His troops. There are exciting twists in how Paul unpacks the story and applies it to the theme of spiritual gifts. Here, the Giver of the gifts is the exalted Jesus (cf. 1 Corinthians 12:4–11, where the Spirit dispenses spiritual gifts). Whereas elsewhere in the New Testament, spiritual gifts are given *to* people; here, the gifts *are* people. The exalted Jesus gives gifted people to the church: "The gifts he gave were that some would be apostles, some prophets, some evangelists, some pastors and teachers" (Ephesians 4:11, NRSV).

The Unified Body of Christ

Paul writes to lay members

When we moved into Cressbrook, we found ourselves living out that old joke about the United States and England being divided by our common language. We had to learn some new vocabulary. On a walk one day, we met some of our new neighbors and learned that those parakeets in their aviary were actually *budgies*. At the market, we found that an eggplant was an *aubergine* and a zucchini was a *courgette*. At home, our baby no longer slept in a crib but in a *cot*, and when we cleaned the carpets, we did not vacuum them but *hoovered* them. What was trickier than learning new words was relearning old ones that now carried very different meanings. *Boot* and *bonnet* were no longer articles of clothing but parts of an automobile. On the other hand, *braces* were no longer medical devices but an article of clothing—suspenders.

Since it is the risen, conquering Jesus who gives us the gifted individuals mentioned in Ephesians 4:11, 12, we must attend carefully to the vocabulary in these verses. Most of the terms sound familiar to us, especially *evangelists*, *pastors*, and *teachers*. We know who those people are. An *evangelist* is a person who holds public evangelistic meetings, inviting people to accept the gospel, embrace the news of Christ's second coming, and become church members. A *pastor* is someone who preaches at church, nurtures the local congregation, and choreographs the congregation's various ministries directed to the community. A *teacher* is someone who teaches in a church school. All of these are professionals, paid employees of the church.

Paul writes to a very different setting, long before the church was organized with conference offices, employees, and paychecks. There existed no clergy over against the laity. The vocabulary is used differently. All of the people Paul mentions—apostles, prophets, evangelists, and pastor-teachers—are church members (what we might today call laypeople) who, in addition to making a living, serve as "ministers of the word." Apostles and evangelists would have an outward focus, seeking to grow the church by drawing community members to faith in Christ. Prophets and pastor-teachers (the Greek syntax suggests one group of people, not two) are focused on the Christian community itself, with prophets sharing messages of divine wisdom, and pastor-teachers nurturing and instructing church members. If we were to look for analogies to our situation today, we might think of these "ministers of the word" as including the personal ministries director, members who lead ministries in the community, elders, and Sabbath School teachers.

Paul is especially interested in a role shared by these lay "ministers of the word" as a group—unifying church members to work for the health and growth of the body (verses 12, 13). Paul worries that church members are not valuing these "ministers of the word" as part of the treasure trove provided by the exalted, conquering Jesus. As a result, he reminds church members of the important, unifying role of these gifted ones. By sharing messages marked by truth and discernment, they recruit and mentor believers, enabling them to contribute to Christian unity, fellowship, and mission (verses 12, 13, 15, 16) and helping them to stay clear of strange winds of doctrine that could destroy their dedication and usefulness (verse 14).

To visualize the unifying role of these "ministers of the word," Paul extends the body metaphor, which he has used earlier (Romans 12:4, 5; 1 Corinthians 12:12–27), in two ways. First, he identifies Christ as the "head" of the body. Instead of falling prey to erroneous doctrines, "we are to grow up in every way into him who is the head, into Christ" (Ephesians 4:15; cf. Colossians 2:19). Second, he identifies the "ministers of the word" as *haphai*, a Greek word that means "ligaments," "tendons," or "joints" (Ephesians 4:16; cf. Colossians 2:19).[5] Apostles, prophets, evangelists, and pastor-teachers play a crucial, unifying role as the connective tissue that unifies the various parts of the body and joins them to the Head of the body, Christ. They are to play this role to help believers grow together toward "mature manhood, to the measure of the stature of the fullness of Christ" (Ephesians 4:13). Since we will pursue that goal until the second coming of Jesus, this description suggests that these types of gifted individuals are to remain active in God's church until then.

We must not miss an overarching, transforming vision Paul offers in his fresh treatment of spiritual gifts. Paul invites us to consider other members of the church from a new vantage point. Too often, we view our fellow church members through the lens of some fault or defect they exhibit. Paul invites us instead to regard each church member both as *gifted* by the Holy Spirit with specific qualities and abilities that can help to nurture the fellowship of believers (verses 7, 16) and as a special, valuable *gift*—one given by the exalted Jesus from His position on the throne of the cosmos (verses 8, 11, 12). Christ is risen! Christ is exalted as Co-regent of the cosmos! Christ has given us valuable, treasured gifts in our fellow church members! We learn to view one another in the light of Christ's exaltation and conquest as part of the treasure trove He has shared with His church.

The Royal Visitor

For some time after we returned from England, we corresponded with one Cressbrook family who had become very special to us: Chris, Jean, and Sophie Holmes. In a Christmas letter, Chris shared news about all our friends in the row of terrace houses where we had lived. In the middle of the letter was a carefully understated announcement: "You may be interested to know that your correspondents have entertained the Duchess of Devonshire for afternoon tea." A brief note. No hint of braggadocio. Beneath that bland statement, we could read the dash of excitement in Chris's eye and the thrill of joy on Jean's face. The Duchess of Devonshire was a noble and the owner of a large portion of County Derbyshire and of Chatsworth House, one of the half-dozen treasure houses in England. In Chris's quiet statement, we could hear the burgeoning joy of sharing their humble habitation with royalty. To have a royal guest present in their home for a few minutes on one afternoon, what a thrill! The privilege of a lifetime!

We believers have the privilege of entertaining a Royal Visitor not simply for an afternoon but as a permanent and friendly house guest. Christ descends to us in the Spirit and dwells "in our hearts through faith" (Ephesians 3:17). He brings gifts to us in the persons of our fellow church members, announcing them as the valuable treasures that they are.

As we nurture His presence in our lives and congregations and benefit from the ministry of our fellow church members, we come to enjoy "the unity of the Spirit in the bond of peace" (Ephesians 4:3) and to experience growing up "into him who is the head, into Christ, from whom the whole body, joined and held together by every joint with which it is equipped, when each part is working properly, makes the body grow so that it builds itself up in love" (verses 15, 16). Such a wondrous reality can plant a dash of excitement in your eye!

---

1. Nonbiblical quotations in this paragraph are from Eugene H. Peterson, *Practice Resurrection: A Conversation on Growing Up in Christ* (Grand Rapids, MI: Eerdmans, 2010), 166, 171.

2. For the categories "ministry of word" and "ministry of deed," see Ronald Y. K. Fung, "Ministry in the New Testament," in *The Church in the Bible and the World*, ed. D. A. Carson (Grand Rapids, MI: Baker, 1987), 154–212.

3. See Charles H. Talbert, *Ephesians and Colossians*, Paideia (Grand Rapids, MI: Baker, 2007), 118, 119.

4. In Paul's citation, Christ "gives gifts." In the Old Testament text, Yahweh is portrayed as "receiving gifts among men." This difference may be due to Paul's creative use of the Old Testament text, his dependence on a different textual tradition, or his use of the wider context of the psalm in which Yahweh "gives power and strength to his people" (Psalm 68:35).

5. Paul uses the term only in the singular, *haphē*, in the phrase "every *joint* with which it is equipped" (Ephesians 4:16; emphasis added; cf. Colossians 2:19, where it is used in the plural).

8

Christ-Shaped Lives and Spirit-Inspired Speech

Ephesians 4:17-32

Perhaps you recall seeing the story on a news website: " 'Swearing at Work Boosts Team Spirit, Morale' "[1] or ". . . $#%&! Researchers Say It's Good to Swear at Work!"[2] These headlines introduced brief summaries of a study done at the University of East Anglia in the UK, "Swearing at Work and Permissive Leadership Culture," published in *Leadership & Organization Development Journal.*[3] "A leadership study found the use of 'taboo language' made the workplace more tolerable," and "regular swearing at work can help boost team spirit among staff, allowing them to express better their feelings as well as develop social relationships."[4] Reader responses were interesting, with some affirming the study's conclusions along these lines: "Swearing is a perfectly natural and legitimate part of any language. When you are around your chums, swear away to your heart's content. It's effective, rewarding communication."

Motives of the heart

How should Christians respond to such a view of human speech? The argument makes some sense, given that no particular string of phonemes is immoral in and of itself. However, in a specific language and cultural setting, we attach meaning to sets of phonemes. From a Christian perspective, God does not ask us to be moral and ethical in only a narrow, abstract sense. We are called, in the specific context of the cultures in which we live, "to do justly, to love mercy, and to walk humbly with . . . [our] God" (Micah 6:8, NKJV). If there is a God, and if that God created us and our capacity for speech, does He offer any advice about how we should manage our speech? Are our chums the only arbiters of what comes out of our mouths? How does God expect us to use His amazing gift of speech?

Paul imagines his Epistle to the Ephesians being read aloud in house churches in greater Ephesus, turning written language into speech. In his letter-speech, he has a great deal to say about harmful speech ("corrupting talk," Ephesians 4:29), such as boasting (Ephesians 2:8, 9), name-calling (verse 11), sharing false doctrine (Ephesians 4:14; 5:6), falsehood (Ephesians 4:25), sexually explicit conversation (Ephesians 5:3, 4), and provoking and threatening others (Ephesians 6:4, 9). He also discusses and exemplifies Spirit-inspired, healthy speech—truth telling that builds up those who hear it (Ephesians 4:25, 29). To speak in such a way is to pattern our speech after Jesus Himself, the Preacher of reconciliation. Like Jesus, we are to preach peace (Ephesians 2:17), a vocation Paul inherits (Ephesians 3:8, 9). In place of damaging speech, such as angry, slanderous outbursts (Ephesians 4:31), Paul offers the replacements of praise to God (Ephesians 1:3–14), tenderhearted words of forgiveness (Ephesians 4:32), thanksgiving and songs of worship addressed to God (Ephesians 5:4, 18–20), and praying for others (Ephesians 6:18–20; a pattern of speech Paul himself repeatedly illustrates [Ephesians 1:15–21; 3:14–21]).

The apostle does not seem too impressed with the let-it-all-hang-out, cuss-away, swear-with-your-chums philosophy of life. Paul argues that the Christian standard of human speech is far more challenging than removing damaging words from our lips. It does not simply scribe the headline "Swearing at Work Is Bad!" It addresses the motives of our hearts and asks us to replace gutter talk with grace-filled speech.

Paul highlights how church members should speak to one another in two important segments of his letter: Ephesians 4:17–32 (the focus of this chapter) and Ephesians 5:1–20 (the focus of the next chapter). In Ephesians 4:17–32, Paul invites his hearers to fully embrace their new lives as Christians, turning away from the coarse, corrupt lifestyles of their past when they lived in ignorance of God (verses 17–19). They have now "learned Christ" (verse 20), how to "put off" the "old self" and "put on the new self, created after the likeness of God in true righteousness and holiness" (verses 22, 24).

This shift means a dramatic metamorphosis in how the hearers speak, leaving behind "falsehood" and replacing it with truth (verse 25). Their transformed speech is motivated by a new reality: they are now "members of one another," parts of the body of Christ, joined together in the church of the Living God (verse 25). These church members, with whom they now share their new lives, are not unrelated, disconnected people to be scolded at will. They are attached to these treasured ones by the most precious bonds of faith. So they must be cautious with anger, which is bound to raise its ugly head. Should they become angry, they must not let it fester but be rid of it by sundown (verse 26; cf. Matthew 5:21–26). Allowing anger to gain a foothold would give the devil an opportunity to damage and disrupt the reconciled fellowship of the church, blood bought by Jesus (Ephesians 4:27; cf. Ephesians 2:11–22).

Spirit-inspired speech

Ephesians 4:29–32 represents one of the most pathos-filled appeals in all of Scripture regarding the use of speech, with each phrase offering valuable counsel. Paul writes, "Let no corrupting talk come out of your mouths" (verse 29; the Greek adjective *sapros* means "rotten" or

---

Does Paul command us to be angry?

In Ephesians 4:26, Paul quotes Psalm 4:4—"Be angry, and do not sin"—a quotation often taken as an exhortation to righteous indignation with a meaning like this: "Go ahead and be angry. Just make sure you are angry for the right reasons." The psalm, though, advocates careful thought, silence, and trust in God (Psalm 4:4, 5). And Paul will shortly ban anger and angry speech (Ephesians 4:31). This suggests that Paul's command should be understood as a concessionary one that could be paraphrased, "Should you become angry, do not allow your anger to bear fruit in full-blown sin." This view—that Paul is interested not in the exercise of anger but in limiting it—is confirmed by his further command, "Do not let the sun go down on your anger" (verse 26).

"decaying"). Paul imagines the destructive word arising in the heart and making its inexorable way toward the lips to do its damaging work. To paraphrase Paul's thought, "When a damaging word rises in your throat, swallow it!" Paul asks believers to adopt an internal, Spirit-inspired interrogation of their speech that applies three criteria before releasing any statement:

1. Is it "good for building up" (verse 29)? Will it encourage or discourage the hearers? Will it build others' faith and fuel their hope?
2. A word may be positive, but does it also fit the occasion (verse 29)? Is it a timely, fitting word? Is it appropriate in the specific context you are about to speak it?
3. The culminating, ultimate test is this one: Would the statement you are about to make "give grace to those who hear" it (verse 29)? Paul

invites us in our speech to model God's treatment of us (verse 32) and convey to others the "grace"—the undeserved favor, blessing, and forgiveness—that God has practiced toward us in Jesus.

Does the word you are about to speak open up fresh, positive trajectories for your hearers? Does it affirm their new, grace-bathed identity in Christ? Paul imagines the Spirit installing this amazing speech filter in our minds: Does my statement build up the hearers? Is it fitting and timely? Does it bless the hearers with grace?

That the installation of this filter is the work of the Holy Spirit is obvious in Paul's next statement: "And do not grieve the Holy Spirit of God, by whom you were sealed for the day of redemption" (verse 30). The "sealing" Paul has in mind here is the one that occurs at conversion, when believers receive the gift of the Holy Spirit, marking them as God's own (Ephesians 1:13, 14). It is intended to be a central marker in the believers' lives until "the day of redemption," the return of Christ. To misuse God's gift of speech to damage others would "grieve" the Holy Spirit, who exhibits an enduring commitment to sharing life with us! To use the gift of speech well is to be alert to the Holy Spirit's winsome presence.

Paul concludes Ephesians 4:17–32 by contrasting the type of speech that should be "put away from you" (verse 31) with the Spirit-inspired speech that should characterize Christian communication. In a list of six vices, Paul describes deep-seated attitudes: "bitterness," "wrath," "anger," and "malice," which he worries will yield the angry speech of "clamor" and "slander" (verse 31). He worries that subterranean, smoldering emotional fires will erupt into flows of molten lava. Deep-seated, destructive attitudes—animosity, rage, and indignation—will, eventually, be expressed through angry shouting and abusive speech, wreaking havoc.

"Slander" or "abusive speech"—bitterness-driven speech intended to damage or destroy someone's reputation with innuendo, half-truths, and outright lies—has no place in Christian discourse. Paul demilitarizes speech as it is to be practiced among Christians. The attitudes that drive angry speech and the rhetorical strategies that reflect it are to be removed from the Christian's arsenal. When these harmful practices are laid aside, Christian community will flourish.

In a final, pathos-filled exhortation, Paul summarizes the Christ-inspired (verse 20), God-imitating (verse 24) pattern of life and speech that he hopes will characterize the Christian house churches in Ephesians: "Be kind to one another, tenderhearted, forgiving one another, as God in Christ forgave you" (verse 32). Vertical forgiveness, which God offers to us, is the model for horizontal forgiveness, which we offer each other. God has been kind, tenderhearted, and forgiving to us; we are to be so to our fellow church members, whatever the form of our communication.

Considering the context of Paul's counsel about speech highlights this truth: When believers use speech to build up people rather than tear them down, they are not simply practicing common Christian courtesy. They participate strategically in God's grand scheme to unify all things in Christ (Ephesians 1:9, 10).

In Ephesians 4:1–16, Paul expands on his central theme of unity by affirming attitudes and behavior that nurture it. With a focus on human speech, he does the same in verses 17–32, identifying divisive behavior that undermines unity (verses 17–19, 22, 25–31) and urging positive, unity-building speech (verses 25–32). By employing unifying speech, believers are to illustrate what it means to be part of the one new humanity—a new way of being human—that God has created out of the disparate parts of humankind (Ephesians 2:11–22). As members of the church, they are signaling to the powers of darkness that God's great plan to unify all things in Christ is underway (Ephesians 3:10). To look ahead to Paul's conclusion, as members of the army of Christ and active combatants in the great controversy, they are deploying speech to proclaim the gospel of peace (Ephesians 6:10–20).

Freed to follow

As we ponder Ephesians 4:17–32, Paul's repeated, forceful exhortations toward unifying speech can take a toll on us. We can begin to feel bombarded by his lists of dos and don'ts. I once heard Dr. Paul Scott Wilson, author of several books about preaching, offer a profound word of counsel to preachers: "Seek the gospel in the text." Where do you find the gospel in a negative command like this: "Let these things be removed from among you: animosity, rage, indignation, angry shouting, and abusive speech, with all ill-will" (verse 31, author's translation)? Just here: Paul does not command us to lift ourselves up by our bootstraps. He points us beyond our own resources to the gracious actions of God in Christ Jesus and to the power and presence of the Holy Spirit in our lives. Every command, you see, is a promise:[5] "Let these things be removed from among you: animosity, rage, indignation, angry shouting, and abusive speech, with all ill-will."

A heavy burden weighs down our hearts. It is a burden of animosity, rage, and indignation. Unfortunately, we have all too often expressed powerful, deep-seated emotions through angry shouting and abusive speech. We see the problem. We feel the massive weight of the burden. It is sinking us. We have put our shoulders to the load. For days, weeks, and years, we have struggled. On occasion, we fantasize that the load budges an inch or two. But it does not. It remains, burdening our hearts, ruining our lives, and sapping our spirits.

Then one day (will it be today?) that great Master of the human spirit, Jesus Christ, appears. "My son," He says, "My daughter, step away from that load. Why, you have been at it for so long that your shoulder is bruised and bleeding!" With some display, He rigs that amazing, cruciform contraption of His—the block and tackle of His

73

grace—above the platform of your life. That heavy burden of animosity, rage, indignation, angry shouting, and abusive speech lifts off your sagging spirit. You are free to follow Him and speak the grace and mercy He has brought into your life.

The power of words

It was the summer of 2014. Islamic State (ISIS) fighters roared into northern Iraq, festooned with AK-47s, waving grenades, brandishing rusty swords, and driving dusty pickups. However, another, more formidable army preceded them—an army of speech conducted on every social media platform available to them, especially Facebook and Twitter. Selfies of black-clad militants. Instagram images of convoys. A smartphone app so people could follow the "progress" of the invasion and link their social media accounts to it.

This digital assault was documented in P. W. Singer and Emerson T. Brooking's 2018 book *LikeWar: The Weaponization of Social Media.* Organized under #AllEyesOnISIS, which became the top-trending hashtag on Arabic Twitter, news of the invasion splashed on millions of screens, including the computers and smartphones of the defenders of the cities that ISIS aimed to conquer. Those defenders heard the demands of ISIS for swift surrender. They watched the gruesome torture and execution of those who dared to resist. To quote Singer and Brooking, #AllEyesOnISIS took on "the power of an invisible artillery bombardment, its thousands of messages spiraling out in front of the advancing force. Their detonation . . . [sowed] terror, disunion, and defection."[6] By the time their ragtag ISIS army of just fifteen hundred militants reached the three thousand-year-old city of Mosul, its defenders and police had largely fled the city, along with half a million citizens. ISIS could not believe its good fortune. "It wasn't a battle but a massacre, dutifully filmed and edited for the next cycle of easy online distribution."[7]

How will you use God's great gift of speech? What will be the effect of the sixteen thousand words you will speak today?[8] When you log on to Facebook, Twitter, Snapchat, or Instagram, or when you dialogue with coworkers, friends, and family, how will you wield your words? Will you follow the way of ISIS, weaponizing your words as acts of war, unleashing death and destruction? Or by the grace and mercy of God, will you hear and follow Paul's Spirit-inspired counsel, speaking "only such as is good for building up, as fits the occasion, that it may give grace to those who hear" (Ephesians 4:29)? Will you invest your words strategically, deploying them to advance God's grand plan to unite all things in Christ, the Prince of Peace?

---

1. " 'Swearing at Work Boosts Team Spirit, Morale,' " *Indian Express*, October 17, 2007, http://archive.indianexpress.com/news/Swearing-at-work-boosts-team-spirit-morale/229366/.

2. Matt Finkelstein, "Holy $#%&! Researchers Say It's Good to Swear at Work!," *Inc.*, October 19, 2007, https://www.inc.com/news/articles/200710/swearing.html.

3. Yehuda Baruch and Stuart Jenkins, "Swearing at Work and Permissive Leadership Culture: When Anti-social Becomes Social and Incivility Is Acceptable," *Leadership & Organization Development Journal* 28, no. 6 (September 2007): 492–507, https://doi.org/10.1108/01437730710780958.

4. " 'Swearing at Work Boosts.' "

5. See Ellen G. White, *Education* (Nampa, ID: Pacific Press®, 2014), 126.

6. P. W. Singer and Emerson T. Brooking, *Likewar: The Weaponization of Social Media* (Boston: Houghton Mifflin Harcourt, 2018), 5.

7. Singer and Brooking, 6.

8. Julie Huynh, "Study Finds No Difference in the Amount Men and Women Talk," University of Arizona Undergraduate Biology Research Program, June 19, 2014, https://ubrp.arizona.edu/study-finds-no-difference-in-the-amount-men-and-women-talk/ (web page is no longer available).

9

Living Wisely

Ephesians 5:1-20

As I passed the display booth, I overheard two attendants. One asked, "Shall we do it now or later?" The other responded, "Let's wait a few minutes." Then came the question, "One dollar or two?" which elicited the response, "Let's go with one dollar." As a college teacher, I regularly attended a large annual meeting of professional organizations. While I valued listening to scholarly papers, I especially enjoyed the extensive convention display hall with exhibits by scores of book publishers. I knew that near the convention's conclusion, publishers would sell off their remaining stock at very low prices. So, on this particular occasion, I arrived a couple of hours before the exhibit hall was to close. As I passed the HarperCollins booth, I heard the exchange between the two attendants. I rapidly scrutinized the expensive volumes in the booth and selected a large stack about two feet high. Then I waited for the announcement, "The books in the HarperCollins booth are now one dollar each!" At that moment, I stepped up to the cash register and made my purchase.

At first blush, Ephesians 5:1–20 may seem like a random, rapid-fire stream of commands directed at believers, "a barrage against sexual license and innuendo."[1] To understand the passage, we need to grasp

Paul's perspective and his tone. The section looks toward the full establishment of "the kingdom of God and Christ" (verse 5), before which "the wrath of God comes upon the sons of disobedience" (verse 6). When Paul describes, in Ephesians 5:15, 16, how believers should live as they look toward the return of Christ, he borrows a word from the marketplace: *exagorazō* (you can see the word for "marketplace," *agora*, in the middle of the word). The verb evokes the moment of frenzied buying when merchandise is offered at steeply discounted prices. It means to "snap up the bargains," and Paul uses it to urge taking full advantage of the opportunities that are on offer as we await Christ's return. "Christian hope is not wishful thinking. Christian hope is an expectant leap forward. We take action. We live in motion."[2] Paul's perspective is that of the end time. He offers counsel for the last days.

This perspective is supplemented by Paul's tone—an urgent one of the battlefield. The passage shows a set of preparation-for-battle themes that Paul has used earlier in Romans 13:11–14 and 1 Thessalonians 5:1–11, as illustrated by table 2:

Table 2. Preparation-for-battle themes

Theme	Rom. 13:11–14	1 Thess. 5:1–11	Eph. 5:1–20	Eph. 6:10–20
Attend to the time: hour, night/day, the unexpected timing of Christ's return, etc.	11, 12	2–4	15, 16	
Awake and/or abandon sleep	11	6, 7	14	
Abandon darkness, works of darkness, believers are not in darkness, etc.	12	4, 5	8, 11	12
Put on armor, or put on the Lord Jesus Christ	12, 14	8		11, 13–17

Walk in the light, live as children of light, believers are children of light, etc.	13	5	8, 9, 13, 14	
Abandon sexual immorality	13, 14		3–6, 11, 12	
Abandon drunkenness and/or be sober	13	6–8	18	
Abandon divisive or crude speech	13		3, 4, 12	
Practice encouraging, unifying speech; prayer; and thankful worship speech		11	19, 20	18, 19
Believers not destined for wrath or destruction, or disobedient destined for wrath		3, 9, 10	5, 6	

In Ephesians 5:1–20, Paul repeats all the earlier preparation-for-battle themes with one notable exception—the call to put on armor, which he reserves for his ringing conclusion in Ephesians 6:10–20. As we study Ephesians 5:1–20, we are already on the battlefield of the cosmic conflict, with Paul thinking of believers as soldiers who are called to a special degree of dedication as they prepare for battle. Our passage is not a random list of exhortations but Paul's end-time battlefield instructions to combatants in the great controversy. In this list, Paul highlights four themes of make-or-break significance: (1) sexual purity in immoral days (verses 3–6), (2) Christian witness in dark days (verses 7–14), (3) discerning God's will in perplexing days (verses 1–20), and (4) strategic worship in evil days (verses 15–20).

Sexual purity in immoral days (verses 3–6)

Paul's tart ban of sexually explicit speech (verse 4) makes it clear that his focus is on the Christian house churches as they gather for worship (verses 18–20). He writes in awareness of the devastating impact that adultery and other forms of sexual immorality could have on the churches in Ephesus, damaging God's grand initiative in establishing the church as a signal of His planned, cosmic unity in Christ (Ephesians 1:9, 10; 2:11–22; 3:10). He dares to offer substitutes to fill any vacuum created by the absence of suggestive speech: "psalms, hymns, and songs from the Spirit" and "giving thanks . . . to God" (verses 19, 20, NIV). Instead of recounting sexual experiences, conquests, and jokes, he imagines songs of praise and thankful speech directed toward God.

Living a life that revolves around sexual sin is more than a threat to the effectiveness and unity of house churches in the present; it imperils future salvation (verse 5). Any who do so fall victim to "empty words" that suggest sexual sin and Christian discipleship may coexist happily in the lives of believers (verse 6). The New Testament bears repeated witness to the attractiveness of sexual sin to some who were tempted to meld a lascivious lifestyle with Christian identity (1 Corinthians 6:12–20; 2 Timothy 3:6; Hebrews 13:4; 2 Peter 2; Jude 4; Revelation 2:14, 20). Paul cautions that believers who are deceived in this way will suffer the same judgment, "the wrath of God," that "comes upon the sons of disobedience" (Ephesians 5:6). Paul earnestly warns believers to avoid both the decimation of church fellowship in the present and the loss of eternal life at Christ's return.

Sexual violence and abuse, often fueled by pornography, are crushing realities that too often invade the current experience of Christian believers. Congregations today have responded to these realities by establishing ministries to aid believers in their struggle against sexual sin and to assist victims of sexual violence and abuse. One could argue that since Paul bans even the mention of sexual immorality, by definition, such groups must be banned since they must discuss these matters. Such a conclusion would be to misunderstand and misread Paul's urgent counsel. He opposes advertising sexual sin, recruiting believers to deny their commitment to Christ by participating in it. Ministries that seek to help believers recover from sexual addictions and the misuse of human sexuality are doing the Lord's work and need not fear Paul's censure.

Rather than dodging or diffusing Paul's message, the realities of our time call us to acknowledge his pressing counsel as appropriate to our engagement in the cosmic conflict. We must make his counsel the subject of earnest self-examination and prayer.

Christian witness in dark days (verses 7–14)

In another word of critical battlefield advice, Paul calls believers to bear witness to their faith in dark days, in a time marked by "the works of darkness" (verse 11). Declaring that believers are "light in the Lord," he charges them to "walk as children of light," living out what they discern to be "pleasing to the Lord" (verses 8–10). Beyond avoiding "works of darkness" and acts too shameful to be mentioned, believers are to "expose" such deeds (verses 11, 12). Paul cryptically and poetically refers to how they are to do so: "But when anything is exposed by the light, it becomes visible, for anything that becomes visible is light" (verses 13, 14). He does not envision harsh, public confrontation with their pagan neighbors. He imagines instead that they will employ a strategy of showing forth God's goodness for engaging unbelievers, exhibiting the alternative of a righteous, God-honoring lifestyle for all to see. Such a witness holds the promise of light-bathed transformation.

Paul concludes his call for Christian witness in dark days by citing a saying or hymn: "Awake, O sleeper, and arise from the dead, and Christ will shine on you" (verse 14). In this saying, is Paul addressing the unbeliever, inviting such a one to respond positively to the Christian's witness? Or is he addressing the believer who is reticent to show forth the light of the gospel? Probably the latter, since Paul draws on Isaiah 60:1–3, which is addressed to God's people. If so, the statement offers a heartwarming promise: As you seek to bear witness to Christ in difficult times, Christ Himself will inspire and encourage you. The light you share will be refracted light, originating in the light Christ shines into your life.

Discerning God's will in perplexing days (verses 1–20)

Paul twice commends an important end-time task: (1) "try to discern what is pleasing to the Lord" (verse 10), and (2) "understand what the will of the Lord is" (verse 17).

Paul's repeated exhortation offers insight into the age-old question, How do I know the Lord's will for my life? Understanding God's will does not (at least usually) happen in a momentary flash of insight; it is a process of thought, discernment, and testing (verse 10), leading to a decision about the values that will determine one's choices (verse 17).

Ephesians 5:1–20 suggests useful strategies that inform the process of discerning God's will:

1. Observe the Pattern carefully (verses 1, 2). We are to be "imitators of God" and of Christ (verse 1), patterning our lives after the God of love and the self-sacrificing Christ.

2. Reflect on the lifestyles of unbelievers as exhibits of how not to live (verses 3–18). Paul develops this thought in detail, pointing to sexual immorality (verses 3–6); crude speech (verse 4); ignorance or disdain of God and His coming judgment (verses 5, 6); fruitlessness (that is, unbelievers live self-centered lives, failing to serve God or others; verse 11; cf. verse 9); secretive, shameful sin (verse 12); lack of wisdom, or foolishness (verses 15, 17); and the use and abuse of alcohol (verse 18; see "Excursus: Wine and Drunkenness in Ephesians 5:18" below).

3. Learn with fellow believers (verses 19–21). Decisions about God's will are not intended to be lonely, individual ones. The process of discerning God's will is advanced by worshiping with other believers, seeking their counsel, and submitting to the wisdom God shares through them (verses 19–21).

Excursus: Wine and drunkenness in Ephesians 5:18

It is often assumed that in his exhortation "Do not get drunk with wine" (Ephesians 5:18), Paul does not speak against drinking wine but is opposed only to becoming drunk as a result of drinking wine to excess. The command is then taken to mean that it is OK to drink wine. Is this an appropriate understanding?

Two arguments suggest this view is inadequate:

1. Paul's injunction quotes Proverbs 23:31, "Do not get drunk with wine," signaling that he is drawing on the treatment of intoxicating beverages in Proverbs 20:1 and 23:29–35. These wisdom passages locate the evil associated with wine and strong drink not just in the drunkenness that results from consuming it but in the drink itself: "Wine is a mocker, strong drink a brawler" (Proverbs 20:1). Danger is present from the moment the cup is lifted toward one's lips: "Do not look at wine when it is red, when it sparkles in the cup and goes down smoothly" (Proverbs 23:31).

Paul reflects this line of thinking, associating "debauchery" with the wine itself. This is masked by translations such as the ESV: "And do not get drunk with wine, for that [i.e., getting drunk] is debauchery" (Ephesians 5:18). However, in Greek, "debauchery" is attached to the wine itself (given that the preceding relative pronoun, "which," agrees in number, gender, and case with the noun "wine"). A more accurate translation of the Greek would be, "And do not get drunk with wine, in which [i.e., in the wine] is debauchery." Mirroring Proverbs, Paul warns against the risks associated with imbibing wine.

---

2. As table 2 shows, Ephesians 5:1–20 reflects terms and ideas Paul has already used in Romans 13:11–14 and 1 Thessalonians 5:1–11. Both passages encourage believers, cast as soldiers preparing for battle, not to be drunk but rather to be sober, drawing a sharp contrast between the two behaviors. Drinking wine (which Paul does not mention in Ephesians 5:1–20) and drunkenness (which he does) are, in the context of the culture of the time, nighttime behaviors (Romans 13:13; 1 Thessalonians 5:7). Christian believer-soldiers need to wake up to their identity as children of light (Romans 13:12; 1 Thessalonians 5:5), who are outfitted in "the armor of light" (Romans 13:12) and who practice behavior that is proper for "the daytime" (verse 13). "Since we belong to the day, let us be sober," fully alert and fully armed and prepared for spiritual battle (1 Thessalonians 5:8; cf. verses 5, 6). Paul wishes Christian believers to be as stone-cold sober as someone who has just awakened (cf. "fully sober," 1 Peter 1:13, NIV), ready for their battle-like engagement in Christian discipleship.

In view of these two arguments, which of the following two positions aligns more closely with Paul's command? (1) Paul is only concerned about drunkenness and approves the consumption of wine. Believers may, with perfect propriety, drink wine as long as they avoid getting really drunk. (2) There is an inherent danger in drinking wine. The Christian believer should be on the alert and be careful to practice sobriety.

Strategic worship in evil days (verses 15–20)

The book of Revelation invites earthlings to practice tactical, battle-field worship of God (e.g., Revelation 14:6, 7). "Worship in the last days becomes a strategic issue. The book unveils overall a cataclysmic conflict being waged across the expanse of heaven and earth as to *who* is to be worshiped, Satan the Deceiver or the Lord God."[3] Paul concludes the battlefield instructions of Ephesians 5:1–20 with a similar call to essential worship (verses 18–20), inviting believers to attend to two important directives from our Commander in Chief: First, do not live life in an alcohol-induced fog (verse 18; again, see "Excursus: Wine and Drunkenness in Ephesians 5:18"). Second, practice instead purposeful, Spirit-inspired worship (verses 19, 20). These commands fit the context of ancient battle well since soldiers preparing for battle were often commanded to be sober and were called to take part in prebattle worship of the gods.

In calling believers to avoid drunkenness and debauchery, Paul urges them to make an end-time substitution for the elaborate dinner and drinking parties—the *symposia*—that were the focus of social life and entertainment at the time. Audaciously, he advocates shared Christian worship as that substitute. Instead of groveling clients offering long, windy speeches to honor their patron and host, we hear energized, joyful, and heartfelt words of thanksgiving "to God the Father in the name of our Lord Jesus Christ" (verse 20). Instead of a caste system descending from the wealthy, dominating host to the abject, impoverished slave, we have the mutual submission practiced by Christian believers (verse 21).

In putting forward his substitute for immoral parties, Paul offers us an inviting and challenging model of Christian worship—one that holds the promise of meeting the deepest longings of human hearts and competing successfully against the practices and attractions of our own time. We have very few sketches of early Christian worship, and we should attend carefully to this urgent call to worship. For Paul, these are the essential characteristics of worship:

1. *Worship is not a spectator sport but is highly participatory.* Paul portrays believers as "filled with the Spirit, addressing one another" in worship (verses 18, 19).
2. *Worship offers varied types of heartfelt, God-centered music.* "Psalms

and hymns and spiritual songs, singing and making melody to the Lord with your heart" (verse 19).

3. *Worship is not a public relations event, advertising the church and its programs.* It is exclusively focused on the worship of God: "Giving thanks always and for everything to God the Father in the name of our Lord Jesus Christ" (verse 20).

Thanksgiving is wonderfully appropriate for end-time Sabbath worship. The fourth commandment (Exodus 20:8–11; Deuteronomy 5:12–15; see also Exodus 20:2; Deuteronomy 5:6) identifies the Sabbath as a day to cease from our labors and celebrate the creative and redemptive acts of God. The Sabbath reminds us that all ultimate blessings—our very existence, redemption, freedom, and rest—are not the result of our work but are the product of God's actions on our behalf. The Sabbath imposes limits on our grinding toil and allows margin to celebrate and live into God's creative and redemptive acts. It does not commemorate our effectiveness but God's grace. The Sabbath is a celebration of the gospel.

Paul imagines Christian believers gathering on the Sabbath to share worship marked by giving thanks to God for who He is and for His grand blessings (Ephesians 5:19, 20). Having given thanks to God in Sabbath worship, we return to the battlefield of the cosmic conflict and of life buoyed by reminders of God's gracious acts in our past and His interest and watch care in the present. We go forth to fight in His armor, with Paul's exhortation echoing in our hearts: "Finally, be strong in the Lord and in the strength of his might" (Ephesians 6:10).

4. *Worship nurtures and actualizes Christian camaraderie and community.* "Submitting to one another out of reverence for Christ" (Ephesians 5:21). For Paul, battlefield worship is shared, corporate worship, which he considers an essential survival strategy for evil, end-time days.

In these last days, as the climax of the great controversy approaches, we have the privilege of joining believers across the ages in the quest for pure devotion to the exalted Jesus, effective witness about Him, and spiritual discernment from Him, all motivated by transformative, end-time worship of our risen, exalted, and returning Savior.

---

1. Ernest J. Bursey, "Paul Talks About Bad Sex," *Collegiate Quarterly* 9, no. 1 (January–March 1986): 91.

2. Jay Y. Kim, "Hope: An Expectant Leap," *Christianity Today*, November 2020, 63.

3. Barry Liesch, *People in the Presence of God: Models and Directions for Worship* (Grand Rapids, MI: Zondervan, 1988), 233, 234; emphasis in the original.

10

Husbands and Wives: Together at the Cross

Ephesians 5:21-33

David, a Jewish slave in a Gentile household in Ephesus, has come to admire another, younger Jewish slave in the same household. Susanna was purchased a few years back, before the whole family became followers of the Way. Snatches of conversation have suggested that Susanna welcomes his feelings for her. So, planning the timing carefully, he requests a meeting with the master and humbly offers his request. Could he and Susanna become husband and wife? He asks the question knowing what it means— their hoped-for "marriage" would not be officialized in any way. It would be informal, completely subject to the master's whims and wishes. Their demanding work for the master would leave little time for themselves. Any children he and Susanna might have would themselves be slaves, the property of their master, and subject to being sold whenever he wished. Still, as David awaits the response, his love for Susanna is strong, and his hopes are high.

* * * * *

Paul's counsel to husband and wives in Ephesians 5:21–33 is the first part of his "household code," which also addresses relationships between children and parents (Ephesians 6:1–4) and between slaves and slave masters (verses 5–9; cf. Colossians 3:18–4:1; 1 Peter 2:13–3:7). The theme of household management was a common one in the literature of the day. To cite one example, Sirach, a Jewish document (ca. 198–175 BC), advises husbands, "Do you have a wife who pleases you? Do not divorce her; but do not trust yourself to one whom you detest" (Sirach 7:26). It advises fathers concerning the treatment of a son: "He who loves his son will whip him often"; "pamper a child, and he will terrorize you; play with him, and he will grieve you"; and "discipline your son and make his yoke heavy, so that you may not be offended by his shamelessness" (Sirach 30:1, 9, 13). With regard to slaves, the document counsels, "Fodder and a stick and burdens for a donkey; bread and discipline and work for a slave"; and "yoke and strap will bow the neck [of an ox], and for wicked slaves there are racks and tortures" (Sirach 33:25, 27).[1]

Like the author of Sirach, most authors wrote only to the husband, father, and slave master in this tone: "Here is how to treat those around you in order to pump up your authority, reputation, and honor." Paul's take is radical, edgy, and different. He addresses everyone: "Here is how to treat those around you the way Jesus has treated you." When set in the context of other counsel available at the time, Paul's advice in Ephesians 5:21–6:9 radiates respect and care for wives, children, and slaves in the framework of loyalty to Christ.

A new way of being human

Paul does not just critique the flawed social structures of the old humanity (Ephesians 4:22). He celebrates the creation of a new humanity (Ephesians 2:15)—a new way of being human that turns away from the corrupt values believers once endorsed. Those old values were characterized by alienation from God and domination by the powers of darkness and driven by the passions of the flesh expressed in sexual abuse and the misuse of speech to berate and devalue others (Ephesians 2:1–3; 4:17–5:17). This new humanity, the church, operates on the basis of new values and rules rooted in God's actions in Christ.

This new way of being human does not exist in the abstract but is embedded within wider humanity with its flawed social structures. From within these structures, believers demonstrate that a new power, the Holy Spirit (Ephesians 2:22; 3:16; 5:18–21; 6:17, 18), and a new, cruciform ethic patterned on Christ (Ephesians 4:13, 15, 20–24, 32; 5:2, 10, 17, 21–33), have been unleashed in the world, pointing toward the fulfillment of God's ultimate plan that the self-giving and self-sacrificing Christ will Himself be the Head of all things (Ephesians 3:8–12; 1:9, 10). In this new humanity, under the sway of the Spirit, those in positions of authority no longer operate to enhance their own power and comfort. They no longer misuse and abuse their charges at will but reflect the self-giving, self-sacrificing model of Christ (Ephesians 5:2, 23, 25, 29). In sharp contrast to other authors, Paul urges believers to live in a countercultural way, against the norms and expectations of society, expressing the newness of the Christian life and unifying the believing community.

Caring and nurturing

The key to understanding and applying Paul's counsel to wives and husbands in Ephesians 5:21–33 is to watch him build toward his quotation of Genesis 2:24: "Therefore a man shall leave his father and mother and hold fast to his wife, and the two shall become one flesh" (Ephesians 5:31). Given his opening exhortation to wives to submit to their "own husbands" because "the husband is the head of the wife" (verses 22, 23), it might seem more appropriate for Paul to have chosen Genesis 3:16, which is a divine word spoken to humankind after the Fall: "Your desire shall be for your husband, and he shall rule over you"

(NRSV). His choice of a pre-Fall word of advice to Adam and Eve in pristine Eden and its strategic, concluding role in the passage suggests that he is building toward a different conclusion.

This thought—that Paul's citation of Genesis 2:24 is especially important to his thinking in Ephesians 5:21–33—is supported by watching him develop the idea of the "one fleshness" of husband and wife throughout the segment. Having identified the husband as the "head" of the wife, Paul expands, "even as Christ is the head of the church, his body" (verse 23). This expansion signals that "head" and "body" are to be understood in the context of a body metaphor: as the head is connected to the body and the body to the head, just as closely is Christ connected to His church, forming a single entity. By implication, the same is true of husband and wife. Paul is already introducing the idea that husband and wife are one body, one flesh.

As Paul turns to counsel husbands, he builds his case toward a one-flesh model of Christian marriage at every turn. In amplifying the example of Christ's relationship to His church (verses 25–27), he suggests that Christ's self-sacrificial attentions to the church as a bride are also appropriately self-serving. The goal of all the bridal preparation of washing, clothing, and adorning that He initiates is the presentation of the bride by Him and to Him. The Husband's reputation and honor are magnified by a beautiful (the word Paul uses is *splendid*) and beautifully clothed bride, perfumed and adorned, standing by His side as the wedding postlude begins. What He does for her, He does for Himself. Christ as Groom prepares the church as a bride for Himself.

In verses 28–30, Paul spells out unequivocally the thought that in caring for the wife, the husband is nurturing himself: "So husbands also ought to love their own wives as their own bodies. He who loves his own wife loves himself" (verse 28, NASB). Paul then offers a further argument in favor of this idea—a general observation or maxim about human life: "For no one ever hated his own flesh, but nourishes and cherishes it" (verse 29). It is as though Paul says, "If my theological reflections about Christ and the church do not move you, let me point out that this is a matter of simple logic." He argues, "As a general rule, we all take good care of our bodies, guarding ourselves against pain and abuse. Since you and your wife are one, the very same rule applies to her. Why would you harm her? In harming her, you are damaging yourself! If you wish to have a truly successful Christian marriage, follow good common sense and the example of Christ, who nourishes and cares for the church."

One flesh

Paul reaches the apex of his argument, the point to which he has been building, by quoting Genesis 2:24 from the Greek Old Testament (the Septuagint or LXX): "Therefore a man shall leave his father and mother and hold fast to his wife, and the two shall become one flesh" (Ephesians 5:31). He means for the quotation to offer scriptural confirmation of his conclusions about Christian marriage. In the setting of the Creation story, Genesis 2:24 teases out the implications of God's creation of woman, "a helper fit for him" (Genesis 2:18), from a rib taken from Adam. When God brings her to Adam, he calls her "bone of my bones and flesh of my flesh," naming her "Woman, because she was taken out of Man" (verse 23). Paul's quotation evokes this full story in which, originating in one flesh, husband and wife are destined to be one flesh.

In quoting Genesis 2:24, Paul argues that the one-flesh model of Christian marriage he is setting forth is embedded deeply in the Creation story and the purposes of God for humankind. For Paul, the statement from Eden that husbands and wives are to be one flesh harbors important wisdom, "a great mystery," referring to "Christ and the church" (Ephesians 5:32, NRSV). "Mystery" does not refer to some profound but still hidden truth but to the topic he has been discussing—a double metaphor with Christian marriage understood in the light of Christ's relationship with His church and Christ's relationship with His church understood in the light of Christian marriage.

Just here, we begin to feel a certain tension as we explore Paul's message about Christian marriage in Ephesians 5:21–33. A vision of trim lawns, white picket fences, and ideal marriages comes into view. Is there any room in the one-flesh model of marriage for my imperfect one? Does the idea of a marriage that echoes God's Creation purpose and mirrors the love of Christ for His church have any place in the real world? While Paul does paint the ideal model for marriage, he does so for a purpose—to invite all of us who are part of imperfect relationships to take a step toward it.

Paul leaves hints that the Christian husbands and wives he addresses are navigating marriage in less-than-ideal circumstances. The husbands he has in mind seem inclined to abuse their wives, too ready to exercise the near-total authority society granted them (verses 25, 28–30). The temptations of adultery and other forms of sexual immorality hover close at hand (verses 3–11). The Christ-saturated, grace-filled gospel in Ephesians applies to real marriages and families. Imperfect though they may be, their families have become part of God's grand family (Ephesians 1:5; 2:19). God is the *Patēr* (Father), "from whom every family [*patria*] in heaven and on earth is named" (Ephesians 3:15). He lays claim to their imperfect families and to ours, including us in the wide circle of His family and His grace.[2] He is drawing your family into His grand plan for the universe, to unify all things in Christ (Ephesians 1:9, 10). He is calling you to join Him in imagining your family as part of that grand plan. What would it look like to take a step toward one-flesh unity (Ephesians 5:21–33), toward the peace and reconciliation of Calvary (Ephesians 2:15, 16), amid the realities of your family circle?

Union, not dominance

In the concluding summary of his counsel to wives and husbands, Paul teases out the practical implications of the one-flesh model for Christian marriage. First, he summarizes his counsel to Christian husbands: "Let each one of you love his own wife as himself" (Ephesians 5:33, author's translation), affirming the importance of the one-flesh model of marriage as the heart and culmination of his logic. "Gentlemen," Paul says, "since you and your wife are 'one flesh,' here is my best counsel to you: Love your wife. Do not just love her in some distant and abstract way. Love her through your kind attentions to her." Next, Paul summarizes his counsel to Christian wives, a summary that should be read in the context of the honor-shame culture of the time: "Let the wife see that she respects her husband" (verse 33). Just as the church should be a credit to her Divine Bridegroom, responding with thankfulness to His kind attentions to her, the wife should respond to her husband's attentiveness with appropriate respect and honor.

What would it mean to take seriously the one-flesh model of Christian marriage that Paul argues in such a detailed way? Two models of Christian marriage have been much discussed in recent times: (1) the complementarian model, which looks to Creation as establishing enduring, complementary roles for men and women in marriage; and (2) the egalitarian model, which also looks to Creation, for an enduring understanding of the equality of husbands and wives. Interestingly, both models tend to focus on the husband over against the wife and vice versa. What if we brought the one-flesh model alongside these two models, hearing the echo of this enduring word, "Therefore a man shall leave his father and mother and hold fast to his wife, and the two shall become one flesh"? What would the one-flesh model accent? It might worry less about roles assigned to one partner in contrast to the other or about measuring the level of equality between the two. Instead, it would focus on who they are together; what they can do and be together; how they can help, nurture, encourage, and respect each other because, from the divine perspective, they are one.

Paul intentionally chooses the pre-Fall standard of Genesis 2:24 for Christian relationships between husbands and wives. By divine design, marriage is intended to be a one-flesh relationship, with sexual unity mirrored in emotional and spiritual unity and emotional and spiritual unity bringing meaning to the sexual relationship. The rampant pornographic exploitation of sexual relationships reveals how deeply rooted in modern culture is the idea of sex as the subjugation of the woman. Paul argues that the sexual relationship, as mirrored in Genesis, is not one of subjugation but of union. It does not symbolize or actualize the dominance of the male but the union of husband and wife, so much so that they are "one flesh." We may look to the passage for a profound countercultural and corrective theology of marriage and sexuality. When we move toward the one-flesh model of marriage, we hear the echo of God's Creation purpose, mirror Christ's relationship with His church, and participate in God's plan for the universe, to unify all things in Christ.

* * * * *

With the master's approval, David and Susanna hope for a few words about their new relationship and a prayer of blessing at the next house church assembly. They are surprised to learn that a guest, Tychicus, is present and are dumbfounded to hear words about Christian marriage from the apostle Paul himself. Stunningly, he does not just talk about the legally and socially sanctioned marriage between their master and mistress. David and Susanna hear Paul speak a scriptural word from Eden over their marriage, "Therefore a man shall leave his father and mother and hold fast to his wife, and the two shall become one flesh." Holding hands, they cry quietly in a corner of the courtyard.

When he has finished reading Paul's letter, Tychicus, with a smile on his face and a twinkle in his eye, says, "Now, I hear that a celebration is in order. Could I ask David and Susanna to come forward, please?" Loud clapping and cheering accompany their embarrassed trek to the front of the colonnade. Motioning them to kneel, Tychicus places his hands on their heads and prays that the Lord Jesus Christ will bless their marriage and that they might love each other just as Christ treasures and nurtures His church. Moved and gratified beyond words, David and Susanna rise and embrace, with their tears now flowing freely.

---

1. All quotations from Sirach are from the NRSVUE. Sirach is less harsh about slaves in Sirach 7:20, 21: "Do not abuse slaves who work faithfully. . . . Let your soul love intelligent slaves; do not withhold from them their freedom," and in Sirach 33:31: "If you have but one slave, treat him like a brother."

2. See John McVay, "How to Enjoy Your Imperfect Family," in *Building Family Memories: Adventist Family Ministries 2015 Planbook*, ed. Elaine Oliver and Willie Oliver (Silver Spring, MD: Department of Family Ministries, General Conference of Seventh-day Adventists, 2014), 25–29.

11

Practicing Supreme Loyalty to Christ

Ephesians 6:1-9

Eight-year-old Ayham Azad knows what it is like to be both a child and a slave. In a televised interview, he was by turns somber and animated with joy. Such joy was remarkable, given all he had been through. When he was four years old, he watched as his Yezidi village in northern Iraq was attacked and his family members were executed by devotees of ISIS, who then kidnapped him.

Taken to Raqqa, he was sold as a slave to Moussa, an ISIS fighter, and Moussa's American wife, Sam. For a couple of years, Ayham lived with the family, learning English and winning a friend in Yusef, Sam's son. While Sam and Yusef befriended him, he experienced the harsh reality of being a slave at the hands of Moussa. He was trained to fire guns and forced to participate in filming an ISIS propaganda video. With the family, he endured the heart-pounding panic of bombings by the US coalition. Ayham responded affirmatively to the question, "Did living with ISIS scare you?" The interviewer followed up by asking, "Why?" Ayham grimly replied, "It scared everybody, not just me. Every day they're killing people. Yeah, every day, every time."[1]

Children and slaves in Ephesus

We are dreadfully wrong if we imagine that we live in a world where slavery is abolished and children are treated with uniform care and respect. When Paul addresses relationships between children and parents and slaves and slave masters, he speaks to a cultural setting that, like our own world, is complex. To be a child in first-century Ephesus was a challenging assignment. Some 3 percent of the population lived lives of abundance, for which the famous terrace houses of Ephesus provide impressive evidence. The rest of the population—the 97 percent—lived just above, at, or below the subsistence level. Among the realities of the time were high rates of infant mortality, which influenced placing a low value on infants. Fathers had the legal right to "expose" a newborn, leaving the infant in the open to die or be "adopted" by a slave trader. This right was often exercised in the case of newborn girls, especially by the poor. Child mortality rates were also high, with only half of children surviving until the age of five.

Children of slaves lived particularly challenging and insecure lives. By birth, they were themselves slaves. The relationship between their parents was informal, subject to the will of the master, as was their own attachment to their nuclear family since they could be sold at any time. Expected to work from an early age, they had little to look forward to except a life of toil. They were completely under the thumb of the slave master, subject to his every command. The master even controlled the sex lives of slaves and could demand sexual favors from them for himself or for whomever he wished.

While some household slaves could hope for freedom, or manumission, around the age of thirty, this was an advanced age at a time when life expectancies were shorter than modern life expectancies. Moreover, with so-called freedom, a slave would become a "freedman," which hardly resembled the existence of a freeborn person. The manumitted slave retained a durable, demeaning identity as a slave as well as a continued relationship with the former master, who could still require various tasks from them and could revoke their manumission if it was economically advantageous to do so.[2]

To children and parents: Remember Jesus

The sketch above casts the form and content of Paul's counsel to children and parents and to slaves and slave masters in high relief since the burden of his message to fathers and slave masters is not to reinforce and augment their power, which was the usual approach of the time. Instead, he brings the tender values of the gospel and especially loyalty to *the* Father and *the* Master to bear upon how fathers and masters will behave. In his strongly countercultural advice, Paul does not speak only to fathers *about* children, as was true for the moralists of the time, but he also speaks *to* children. Paul writes these words to be read aloud in Christian house churches, knowing that children will be present. By speaking directly to them, he honors them, acknowledging them as participants in early Christian worship and as members of the Christian family.

In asking children to obey their parents, he adds a weighty phrase: "Children, obey your parents *in the Lord*" (verse 1; emphasis added). Paul acknowledges children as believers themselves. They are disciples of the Lord Jesus Christ (since "Lord" in Ephesians regularly designates Jesus). They are to think about how they relate to their parents in the context of an even more important relationship—their relationship with the exalted Jesus.

To support his exhortation to children, Paul quotes the fifth commandment, "Honor your father and your mother," breaking into the quotation to offer a remark, "this is the first commandment with a promise," before concluding the quote, "that it may go well with you and that you may live long in the land" (verses 2, 3, quoting Exodus 20:12; cf. Deuteronomy 5:16). He speaks directly to children, sharing a promise-harboring commandment. He believes that the commands and promises of the Bible are theirs. He believes that the Lord loves them and wishes good and long lives for them (verse 3).

Can you imagine a couple of children seated near the courtyard fountain, tossing pebbles into it as they listen to Paul's letter? When they hear the word *children*, they pause, stones frozen in hand, catching the tone of respect for them. The whole letter comes alive as they are reminded of the importance of their relationship with Jesus. These brief words to them are not a children's story sandwiched into a letter meant for adults. If Paul is right that they are "in the Lord," it means that they have been "made . . . alive together with Christ," that they have been "seated . . . in the heavenly places in Christ" (Ephesians 2:5, 6), that they have been reconciled "to God in one body through the cross" (verse 16), and all the rest. It is all theirs in Jesus!

To fathers, Paul offers both negative and positive advice. Negatively, they are not to provoke their children, needlessly angering them in order to assert parental authority. Positively, they are to "bring them up in the discipline and instruction of the Lord" (Ephesians 6:4), to offer instruction and admonition that has the Lord Jesus as its focus and benchmark. What is in view is the "teaching and correcting of children through practical example and through words that are aimed at producing lives shaped by the tradition about Christ the Lord." This focus on Christ "would have given the relationship between Christian children and parents a distinctive ethos."[3]

Reviewing Ephesians 6:1–4, we note that Paul begins his counsel to children by arguing their obedience should be "in the Lord" (verse 1) and concludes his advice to parents with the call to Christ-centered child-rearing: "The discipline and instruction of the Lord" (verse 4). He signals, at the beginning and end of the passage, the importance of discerning, honoring, and nurturing the relationship that children have with Jesus.

The story of God calling to the child Samuel is a powerful biblical narrative that affirms our mandate to honor the relationship between children and their God (1 Samuel 3:1–21). It occurred at a time when God did not speak frequently and directly to His people (verse 1). God breaks the fraught silence by whispering three times in the night to a child, breathing his name, "Samuel!" (verses 4–8). At the moment when this happens, Samuel "did not yet know the LORD, and the word of the LORD had not yet been revealed to him" (verse 7). While he is "ministering to the LORD" (verse 1) and sleeps near "the ark of God" (verse 3), he surely knows about the Lord. But there is a difference between *knowing about the Lord* and *knowing the Lord*, and that more profound experience is absent from Samuel's life. Each time God whispers, Samuel throws off the bedcovers and dashes to Eli, offering the polite explanation to the bleary-eyed priest, "Here I am, for you called me" (verses 5, 6, 8).

If there comes a time in every child's life when the Lord begins speaking to their hearts and minds, whispering in the night, Eli offers parents, teachers, and Sabbath School teachers an important example. It takes him a while—just as it takes us time to recognize it—but he eventually "perceived that the LORD was calling the boy" (verse 8). The small caps typeface of LORD in most English Bible translations indicates the holy name for God, "Yahweh." Eli perceives this truth: "Yahweh" is "calling the boy"! We should be alert to that moment in the lives of the children God has entrusted to our care and be in awe at the realization that the Lord of the cosmos is speaking to that child. We must both discern and honor this new reality, just as Eli does. He scripts Samuel's response to the Lord's fourth greeting, telling him to reply, "Speak, LORD, for your servant hears" (verse 9). This time "the LORD came and stood" and called again, "Samuel! Samuel!" Samuel responds as instructed, though he cannot bring himself to use the divine name Yahweh: "Speak, for your servant hears" (verse 10).

The connection is made between Yahweh and the boy. Samuel now knows the Lord. Immediately, the Lord trusts the boy, sharing with the youngster His terrible and irrevocable judgment on the house of Eli, which is the first of many revelations to Samuel (verses 19–21). In accepting Samuel's difficult message, Eli discerns and honors Samuel's relationship with the Lord, just as Paul encourages us to do in Ephesians 6:1–4. Why is this point so important? Because "the one thing that is more important than" our children's obedience to us is "their obedience to the Voice from above."[4]

To slaves and slave masters: Serve Jesus

Paul speaks at greater length to slaves (verses 5–8) than to slave masters (verse 9). In addressing both, he articulates a common theme: Do not forget your most important relationship. You are all—slaves and slave masters alike—slaves of the exalted Christ. In working this theme out for slaves, Paul asks them to make a grand substitution in their thoughts and behaviors: Put the exalted Christ in the place the culture has reserved for your so-called master. Do not just serve him; serve Christ!

Imagine entering your high school physics classroom just in time to hear the principal announce that your teacher is ill and a substitute will be arriving. A long five minutes later, in shuffles the substitute, a disheveled elderly gentleman with wild hair. You glance down at the photo on the cover of your physics textbook and back up at the substitute to confirm that Albert Einstein has just walked into the room!

Paul repeatedly calls for a still more dramatic substitution—Jesus in the place of the slave master!

1. *"Slaves, obey your earthly masters with fear and trembling, with a sincere heart" (verse 5).*[5] To refer to their masters as their "earthly masters" already announces Paul's point—these Christian slaves have not only an earthly master but also a heavenly Master.

2. *Obey "as you would Christ" (verse 5).* It is difficult—impossible even—to serve your fallible, sometimes violent slave master with dedication and devotion. To serve with a "sincere heart," you will need to make an important exchange. Direct your true, heartfelt service to Christ, the heavenly Master, rather than to your earthly one.

3. *Obey "not by the way of eye-service, as people-pleasers" (verse 6).* Do not obey with your eye on the master, seeking to please a mere human who is not your true and ultimate Master.

4. *"But [obey] as slaves of Christ, doing the will of God from the heart" (verse 6).* You have an alternate, truer, and more important identity than being slaves of your earthly master. You are slaves of Christ! Living into that identity, you will be able to serve with a full heart.

5. *Obey, "rendering service with a good will as to the Lord and not to man" (verse 7).* Again comes the replacement—the Lord Jesus in the place of a mere man.

6. *Obey, "knowing that whatever good anyone does, this he will receive back from the Lord, whether he is a slave or is free" (verse 8).* One final time Paul calls for a substitution. Slaves of Christ may look to Christ, rather than the slave master, for the reward for their labor—an idea Paul expands to include everyone.

Having affirmed the principle of acknowledging Christ as the true Master, Paul extends the idea to the experience of slave masters, beginning his advice to them in an astonishing way: "Masters, do the same to them" (verse 9). I can hear a slave master's under-his-breath response as he hears these words from Paul: "What? Am I supposed to treat my slave the way he treats me? What is this world coming to?" For Paul, the relationship between slaves and slave masters is a reciprocal one, founded on the idea of Christ as the true Master of all.

Paul continues, reasoning with slave masters like this: Since you, a slave master, are not the true and final Master, you have no right to threaten your slaves. You share the true Master with your slaves! All of you serve Him, the heavenly Master, who does not traffic in human categories and labels, classifying one as "slave" and another as "master." He is not partial to one over the other! (See verse 9.)

Paul's repeated call to put Christ in place of others echoes across millennia. In our relationships, especially when they chafe and pinch, we may look up, finding fresh orientation and encouragement in acknowledging the exalted Christ. How might I substitute the Lord for the fallible, difficult, or egotistical people in my life? And how might I perceive Christ in those I am tempted to overlook—including child slaves like Ayham Azad—as we move toward Christ's final pronouncement: "Truly, I say to you, as you did it to one of the least of these my brothers, you did it to me" (Matthew 25:40)?

---

1. Josh Baker, director and producer, "Return From ISIS," *Frontline*, December 15, 2020, https://www.pbs.org/wgbh/frontline/film/return-from-isis/. Some details are drawn from other news accounts.

2. In offering this sketch of first-century life, I am indebted to three books in the InterVarsity Press's A Week in the Life Series, all set in the context of first-century Ephesus: Holly Beers, *A Week in the Life of a Greco-Roman Woman* (Downers Grove, IL: InterVarsity, 2019); John Burton, *A Week in the Life of a Slave* (Downers Grove, IL: InterVarsity, 2019); and David deSilva, *A Week in the Life of Ephesus* (Downers Grove, IL: InterVarsity, 2020.)

3. Andrew T. Lincoln, *Ephesians*, Word Biblical Commentary 42 (Dallas, TX: Word Books, 1990), 409.

4. Richard J. Foster, *The Challenge of the Disciplined Life: Christian Reflections on Money, Sex & Power* (San Francisco: Harper & Row, 1989), 234.

5. In quoting Ephesians 6:5–9 here, I am following the 2007 ESV text, which translates the Greek word *doulos* as "slave," rather than the 2016 revision, which uses "bondservant."

12

The Call to Stand

Ephesians 6:10-20, Part 1

General George Washington knows he is outmanned, outgunned, out-trained, and outclassed. Nonetheless, he decides to march his ragtag army through the streets of Philadelphia, attempting a show of force. For this strategy to be effective, he needs the Continental Army to look as smart and powerful as possible. So he exhorts his men to mind the beat of the fife and drum corps accompanying each brigade and step smartly and in rhythm "without dancing along or totally disregarding the music, as too often has been the case."

As he imagines the event and the reactions of the citizens of Philadelphia, he gives one more directive. Each soldier must wear a sprig of greenery in his hat or hair. Why? It will provide a hint of symmetry for troops dressed in a wide array of shabby costumes. More important, that green twig is a symbol of victory. Washington wishes to telegraph to the watching citizens of Philadelphia that whatever their deficiencies, his army is a confident one, marching in a victory parade. So it is that on Sunday, August 24, 1777, as the Continental Army tramps through the streets of Philadelphia, a sprig of greenery is woven in every soldier's hair or pinned to his hat. Victory is in the air![1]

Nearly two hundred years later, New Testament scholar Markus Barth offers an interesting suggestion about Paul's command to believers to "take the helmet of salvation" (Ephesians 6:17): "Most likely, a 'helmet of victory' is in mind which is more ornate than a battle helmet and demonstrates that the battle has been won."[2] The idea was quickly dismissed by scholars who asked, "Did Roman soldiers even have victory helmets?"

Then, in the year 2000, came a fascinating discovery by amateur archaeologists in a pit near Hallaton, England. What appeared at first to be a mass of corroded, mud-caked iron turned out to be the remains of a highly decorated Roman military helmet. Those remains become the focus of a massive, eleven-year-long reconstruction effort—the "micro-excavation, stabilisation and reconstruction" of hundreds of fragments in a "3D jigsaw puzzle."[3] The rust-colored reconstruction is now on view at the Harborough Museum in Market Harborough, England. An artist's rendering shows the Roman victory parade helmet, probably made AD 25–50, covered with silver sheet and decorated in gold leaf. Ornamented with a wreath, it features a goddess on its brow flanked by animals. On a gilded cheekpiece, a Roman emperor rides on horseback with the goddess Victory flying close behind while a captive cowers beneath the horse's hooves.[4]

If Markus Barth's suggestion, informed by archaeological discovery, is correct, Paul calls on believers—the ragtag army, which to the human eye is the underdog in the looming fight—to do something strange. As they enter the fray, they are not to wear the expected, beat-up battle helmet but don the expensive, embellished, pristine, and gleaming helmet usually carefully secured in the barracks, awaiting the victory parade. Why? It signals their confidence in their Commander and the resources He has provided to ensure victory. In advance, before the final victory is won, they are to celebrate the grand triumph to come!

Is Ephesians 6:10–20 an add-on?

In Ephesians 6:10–20, Paul, as a military general, steps onto the battle-field of the great controversy and urges us to be protected in God's "full armor" (Greek, *panoplia*) as we battle for the already victorious King Jesus. Given its rhetorically powerful military imagery, we tend to think of the passage as self-contained, unrelated to the rest of the letter. Can we read Ephesians as a dramatic sketch of the great controversy? In Ephesians 6:10–20, is Paul gathering up the letter's themes and bringing the portrait of the cosmic conflict woven throughout the letter to a satisfying culmination?

Near the beginning of Ephesians, Paul describes what happens after the death and resurrection of Jesus: God then "seated him at his right hand in the heavenly places, far above all rule and authority and power and dominion, and above every name that is named, not only in this age but also in the one to come" (Ephesians 1:20, 21). While that grand scene is hidden from view, it is disclosed in the gospel. Believers have been chosen in Christ "before the foundation of the world," drawn into the drama of the great controversy to act out God's grand plan for the universe "to unite all things in him [Christ], things in heaven and things on earth" (verses 4, 10).

This new, all-consuming allegiance to the exalted King Jesus inevitably puts believers at odds with things on Earth, where "the prince of the power of the air," the devil, holds sway over "the sons of disobedience" (Ephesians 2:2) and where rulers, authorities, and powers who have rebelled against God (Ephesians 1:21) feign that they are in charge. Believers find that they are an underdog army in an apparently uneven war against all the forces of evil. Given that the Ephesians' champion warrior, Paul, is now a prisoner of war, he worries that believers will "lose heart" (Ephesians 3:1, 13). So he writes Ephesians as a battle manual for his wavering army, unpacking the resources that God has provided for them. These include behind-the-scenes intelligence (e.g., Ephesians 1:8–10, 19–23), an already funded, eternal reward for faithful soldiers (Ephesians 6:11, 12), and the Holy Spirit, whose presence among them guarantees that reward "until we acquire possession of it" (verses 13, 14) and who actualizes "the immeasurable greatness" of God's power among them (verses 19; cf. Ephesians 3:13–21).

In their current battles, they are to recall the strange victory of Jesus, who wins on the cosmic stage by dying. His death, through which He storms the city of darkness and breaks down its "wall of hostility" (Ephesians 2:14), results in a peace treaty that benefits believers who become "fellow citizens with the saints" (verse 19). Christ's victory through death is so important that it is commemorated—as was sometimes the case in ancient times—by building a temple to celebrate it, one in which believers are "being built together into a dwelling place of God by the Spirit" (verses 20–22).[5]

Paul celebrates the church, created by God out of diverse segments of humankind, as a new humanity (verse 15). In the cosmic conflict, the church acts out the reconciliation of Christ rather than the racism inspired by the evil powers, signaling the start of God's ultimate plan to unite all things in Christ (Ephesians 1:9, 10). The church's role in the great controversy is to disclose "to the rulers and authorities in the heavenly places" "the manifold wisdom of God" in creating the church, telegraphing that while the Christian army may seem undermanned and outgunned, it is destined for victory while the doom of the evil powers is underway (Ephesians 3:10).

Having begun the first half of the letter by highlighting the exaltation of Christ (Ephesians 1:9, 10, 20–23), Paul begins the second half in the same way by quoting Psalm 68:18: "When he ascended on high he led a host of captives, and he gave gifts to men" (Ephesians 4:8). Christ, behaving as victorious generals do when they ascend in a victory parade to their capital cities, "gave gifts to his people" (verse 8, NIV). He gave apostles, prophets, evangelists, and pastor-teachers to help believers as the body of Christ be united, strong, and mature and in fighting trim (verses 11–16). He then details what unifying behavior looks like (verses 17–32), wishing to avoid giving the devil any opportunity in the fight (verse 27) as we battle toward "the day of redemption" (verse 30).

Throughout the last half of the letter (Ephesians 4–6), Paul sketches out how believers should behave as soldiers of the Lord Jesus, "eager to maintain the unity of the Spirit in the bond of peace" (Ephesians 4:3). As we have seen, Paul offers end-time battlefield instructions to combatants in the great controversy in Ephesians 5:1–20 (see chapter 9, table 2). Paul's thorough use of preparation-for-battle themes—being alert and awake; abandoning works of darkness, sexual immorality, and drunkenness; and practicing unifying speech and prayer—invites us to read the ensuing household code in Ephesians 5:21–6:9 as an invitation to believers to apply their soldierly allegiance to Jesus Christ to their relationships within the family. Following the examples of Jesus (Ephesians 2:14–17; 4:20–24) and Paul (Ephesians 3:1–13), believers illustrate that "among God's new people, there is no place for control, domination, manipulation or exploitation. Rather, mutual respect and service is to be the norm."[6]

Reading Ephesians as a dramatic sketch of the great controversy, we find "a tightly woven narrative structure that is driven by the pattern of divine warfare."[7] We discover that in Paul's battle exhortation in Ephesians 6:10–20, the grand ideas of the letter return: finding power in solidarity with the Lord Jesus; engaging the powers in God's strength; standing unified and firm by being equipped with God's good gifts of truth, righteousness, gospel, peace, faith, victory, and especially the Spirit; all bathed in the prayer Paul has so thoroughly illustrated (Ephesians 1:3–23; 3:14–21). We hear an urgent "call for redemptive creativity on the part of the church—strenuously exercising our imaginations to come up with creative strategies of cruciformity [mirroring Christ's self-sacrifice on the cross] that subvert the corruptions of the powers and open up opportunities for God to work in power."[8]

What about spiritual warfare?

Since Ephesians 6:10–20 aptly summarizes and concludes Paul's letter to the Ephesians, how are we to understand his detailed military metaphor? The passage is often considered one of the most important Bible passages about spiritual warfare, thought of as battling directly with evil spirits who have taken control of someone. What does our passage say about deliverance ministry?

On the one hand, it says surprisingly little. It does portray the close engagement of believers against "the spiritual forces of evil" (verse 12), standing in God's power against them and wrestling with them (verses 11, 12), and even fending off the direct, fiery assaults of Satan himself (verse 16). However, Paul's emphasis is on God's generous provision for victory through His presence and the weaponry of His truth, righteousness, peace, faith, salvation, and the Spirit.

If Ephesians 6:10–20 is the capstone of the letter, we see that Paul has already defined the ways we "put on" this armor. For example, we do so by avoiding "bitterness and wrath and anger and clamor and slander" (all behaviors that one might expect from ordinary soldiers) and instead are "kind to one another, tenderhearted, forgiving one another" (Ephesians 4:31, 32). Paul does not picture in any specific way what would need to happen should a Christian soldier desert the post of duty, join the opposing force, and become possessed by evil spirits.

However, Ephesians 6:10–20 suggests important principles and ideas that should inform such efforts: trusting in the Lord rather than in our own spiritual power to rescue Satan's captives; acknowledging the need for God's provisions for the battle; trusting in the completed victory of Christ (wearing the helmet of victory!); requesting and relying on the presence of *the* Spirit (verses 17, 18); using the promises of God ("the word of God," verse 17), all expressed through "prayer and supplication" to God (verse 18); trusting in the power of the Spirit to convey, interpret, and expand on our requests on behalf of the oppressed ("praying at all times in the Spirit," verse 18; cf. Romans 8:26, 27).

C. S. Lewis's statement about devils is quoted frequently: "There are two equal and opposite errors into which our race can fall about the devils. One is to disbelieve in their existence. The other is to believe, and to feel an excessive and unhealthy interest in them."[9] Christians in the West often think very little about the presence of evil powers and would be perfectly happy to ignore them altogether. However, in the rest of the world (the majority world), the presence of evil spirits is often a part of day-to-day reality, and the need to participate in the delivery of the demon-possessed can be very real. In 2005, the Seventh-day Adventist Church added a twenty-eighth fundamental belief to acknowledge this reality, celebrating that "by His death on the cross Jesus triumphed over the forces of evil. He who subjugated the demonic spirits during His earthly ministry has broken their power and made certain their ultimate doom. Jesus' victory gives us victory over the evil forces that still seek to control us, as we walk with Him in peace, joy, and assurance of His love."[10]

Those of us who have little experience in helping those oppressed by evil spirits should listen carefully to those who do[11] while being attentive to the multitude of other devious and devastating ways in which Satan and his minions work among us ("the schemes of the devil," verse 11) and while being alive to God's gracious provisions to counter them.

Where is Jesus?

The summary of the letter—Ephesians 6:10–20—exhibits an odd feature. The Christ-drenched letter has been shot through with phrases that celebrate our union, participation, identification, and incorporation with Christ: "in Christ," "with Christ," "through Christ," and so on.[12] None of these phrases occurs in Ephesians 6:11–17 as Paul details his military metaphor of the church as a well-equipped army. Does this mean that Paul's conclusion is defective, failing to reflect the central theme of our oneness with Christ? No! Ephesians 6:11–17 works out the overarching thesis statement of verse 10: "Finally, be strong in the Lord [Jesus Christ] and in the strength of his might." Putting on the head-to-toe armor of God is Paul's ultimate illustration of what it means to be "in Christ." "Through their union with Christ, believers share in his armour and have solidarity with him in battle."[13] In advance, before the final victory is won, they celebrate the grand triumph to come!

1. I am dependent on the account of Ron Chernow's *Washington: A Life* (New York: Penguin Press, 2010), 300–311, and, to a lesser extent, on that of Bob Drury and Tom Clavin's *Valley Forge* (New York: Simon & Schuster, 2018), 14–25.

2. Markus Barth, *Ephesians 4–6*, Anchor Bible 34A (Garden City, NY: Doubleday, 1974), 775. In a context of military language, the Greek word *sōtēria*, usually translated as "salvation," may be better rendered as "victory." So, the "helmet of salvation" of Ephesians 6:17 may be understood as the "helmet of victory."

3. J. D. Hill, "Finishing a 2,000 Year-Old Roman Jigsaw Puzzle: The Hallaton Helmet Unveiled," British Museum, World History Lab, https://worldhistorylab .britishmuseum.org/finishing-a-2000-year-old-roman-jigsaw-puzzle-the-hallaton -helmet-unveiled/.

4. Hill. Other similar helmets, discovered elsewhere, are discussed in "Reconstructing the Hallaton Helmet," *Current Archaeology*, February 14, 2012, https://www .archaeology.co.uk/articles/news/reconstructing-the-hallaton-helmet.htm.

5. Timothy G. Gombis, *The Drama of Ephesians: Participating in the Triumph of God* (Downers Grove, IL: InterVarsity, 2010), 86–88, 103–105.

6. Gombis, 176.

7. Gombis, 30.

8. Gombis, 128.

9. C. S. Lewis, *The Screwtape Letters, With Screwtape Proposes a Toast* (New York: Macmillan, 1961), 3.

10. *Seventh-day Adventists Believe: A Biblical Exposition of Fundamental Doctrine*, 3rd ed. (Silver Spring, MD: Review and Herald®, 2018), 151.

11. A helpful set of essays is found in "Spiritual Warfare and the Occult," a special issue of the *Journal of Adventist Mission Studies* 11, no. 2 (2015): https://digitalcommons .andrews.edu/jams/vol11/iss2/17/.

12. I am using the four terms Constantine R. Campbell adopts to express "the full spectrum of Paul's thought" with regard to such phrases as "in Christ." Constantine R. Campbell, *Paul and Union With Christ: An Exegetical and Theological Study* (Grand Rapids, MI: Zondervan, 2012), 29, 30.

13. Campbell, 153.

13

Waging Peace

Ephesians 6:10-20, Part 2

In January 2020, Rob Macaire, British ambassador to Iran, attended a vigil in Tehran for Ukrainian Airlines flight 752 passengers who died when Iranian forces shot down the aircraft. When the event turned into an anti-government protest, Macaire left, threading his way through the streets of Iran's capital toward the British Embassy. En route, an international incident occurred, which British Foreign Secretary Dominic Raab described as a "flagrant violation of international law." What happened? Ambassador Macaire was arrested and accused of organizing the anti-government protest. However, the foreign secretary's strongly worded complaint resulted in Macaire's release after just an hour in custody.[1]

To arrest an ambassador is a big deal. Sparks fly. Red phones ring. Tensions escalate. Voices are raised. Why? When you arrest an ambassador, you do not just incarcerate a single individual; you dishonor an entire nation and its leader, risking reprisal and war.

When Paul, the long-incarcerated ambassador of Jesus, requests the prayers of believers in Ephesus, he imagines a future meeting with the Roman emperor (Ephesians 6:18–20). Nero will be seated on his throne, dressed in regal splendor, symbols of absolute power dripping off him. Into the ostentation of Nero's judgment hall will step the lonely apostle in his tattered prison garb and grinding chain. The emperor, flanked by guards in full military dress and attended by obsequious administrative aides, will aim for the quick dispatch of this troublesome, eccentric holy man.

Paul frames the scene with a dramatic contrast between the apparent (Nero's authority and power) and the real (Christ's authority and power). He will step into the imperial throne room as the authorized ambassador of the Lord of all things and all time. His appearance and chain aside, Paul will have every right to speak boldly, announcing the will of Nero's Boss, the ascended and exalted Jesus. This will be the last call to client king Nero, a gracious embassage by the Lord Jesus Christ, revealing the divine plan for the universe, the gospel. Heaven's red phone is about to ring.

As is often the case, diplomatic efforts are tied to the battlefield. Paul is not only "an ambassador in chains" (verse 20) but also an imprisoned general and leader of the Christian army in Ephesus. As Paul waits to convey Heaven's message to Nero, he shares his marching orders for believers in an eve-of-battle speech in Ephesians 6:10–20, which can be distilled into four simple commands.

Follow the Leader

The first distilled command is this: *Follow the Leader.* "Finally, be strong in the Lord and in the strength of his might. Put on the whole armor of God, that you may be able to stand against the schemes of the devil" (verses 10, 11). As a general, Paul conveys the orders of the true Commander in Chief, who calls us to battle while promising to be with us in the fight. We are to be strong "in the Lord and in the strength of his power" (verse 10, NRSV).

As Paul crafts his battle exhortation, he has many examples from the

Old Testament on which to draw,[2] including Deuteronomy 20:1–4: "When you go out to war against your enemies, and see horses and chariots and an army larger than your own, you shall not be afraid of them, for the LORD your God is with you" (verse 1). Paul echoes those words: "Finally, be strong in the Lord and in the strength of his might" (Ephesians 6:10). In short, *follow the Leader*.

Our Divine Commander blesses us not only with His presence but also with His panoply—His full armor. For a long time, I assumed the phrase "the whole armor of God" meant only "the full armor which God supplies." Then I discovered that Paul is reflecting on Isaiah 59, where God expresses outrage at the injustice and brutality of His own people: "Their feet run to evil, and they are swift to shed innocent blood" (verse 7). God is "appalled that there was no one to intervene" (verse 16, NRSV), so He Himself steps onto the stage of history as the cosmic Warrior and Judge:

> He put on righteousness like a breastplate,
>   and a helmet of salvation on his head;
> he put on garments of vengeance for clothing,
>   and wrapped himself in fury as in a mantle (verse 17, NRSV).

Does that weaponry sound familiar?

God does not supply us with second-rate armor. He provisions us with His own weapons. The command "put on the whole armor of God" (Ephesians 6:11) means to put on God's own armor. Can you imagine God's weaponry failing? The quality of our gear announces the inevitable outcome—victory for Christ and His church. Our Divine Commander blesses us with His presence and His panoply. In accepting and celebrating both, we *follow the Leader*.

Know the foe

Paul's second command is, *"Know the foe."* "Put on the whole armor of God, that you may be able to stand against the schemes of the devil. For we do not wrestle against flesh and blood, but against the rulers, against the authorities, against the cosmic powers over this present darkness, against the spiritual forces of evil in the heavenly places" (verses 11, 12).

In battle, it will never do to underestimate the opposing forces. Paul invites a realistic assessment. While we confront enemy forces on the human plane, our real battle is with "the spiritual forces of evil in the heavenly places." In according titles of power to the church's spiritual foes, Paul displays a kind of respect for them. There is wary acknowledgment, too, in his description of the devil as a cunning, devious foe. We need God's armor to counter "the schemes of the devil" (verse 11).

However, Paul also offers subtle contempt for Satan, "the evil one": "In all circumstances take up the shield of faith, with which you can extinguish all the flaming darts of the evil one" (verse 16). Paul portrays "the evil one" as an archer, a missile thrower, consistently viewed with contempt in ancient battle literature. In Homer's *Iliad*, Diomedes taunts the archer Paris: " 'You archer, slanderer, proud of your lovely locks. . . . If you were to make trial of me in hostile combat with real weapons and armor, neither your bow nor your thick-showered arrows would do you any good at all. . . . I have no more concern than if a woman or a witless child had struck me.' "[3]

When Paul portrays Satan as an archer lobbing flaming missiles, he paints him as a coward. "The evil one" is fearful of close-order combat. He trembles to confront Christ's gospel army, who are well equipped from God's own armory. Obedient to their glorious Commander in Chief, the united force of believers is to be feared, and the evil one does so. Proving himself the coward, he lobs missiles from afar.

Paul offers, then, a balanced portrait: we must not underestimate the foe as though we face mere flesh and blood but rulers, authorities, and cosmic powers over this present darkness, spiritual forces of evil in the heavenly places—all led by a wily, calculating leader, the "evil one," the "devil." However, the devil is also a coward who fears confrontation with Christ and His church. Trusting in the Commander in Chief, victory is to be expected against this scheming and cowardly foe.

Join the army

Paul issues a third command: *Join the army.* Our passage has usually been taken as a description of the individual Christian's battle against evil. However, in Ephesians 3:10, Paul has the church as a whole engaged with the powers, arguing that "through the church the manifold wisdom of God" is "made known to the rulers and authorities in the heavenly places." The church, says Paul, is a well-equipped, united army fighting in the long-running battle of the cosmic conflict.

Just as soldiers are to support and encourage each other to fight courageously, so believers are called to Christian community and collaboration; this lesson is illustrated by a case study from Paul's letter to the Philippians. The story has filtered its way to him in prison. Two important leaders in the church at Philippi have fallen out with each other, exhibiting the destructive forces of "rivalry" and "conceit" (Philippians 2:3, HCSB). Euodia and Syntyche were once unified members of Paul's missionary team, who "labored side by side" with Paul "in the gospel" (Philippians 4:3). They were soldiers in the army of Christ, "standing firm in one spirit, with one mind striving side by side for the faith of the gospel, and not frightened in anything" by their "opponents" (Philippians 1:27, 28). Now, though, Euodia and Syntyche are fighting each other when they should have been fighting alongside each other. They have made a classic strategic blunder—mistaking an ally for an enemy. In the process, they are destroying the unity of Christ's militia, the church.

Our passage does not portray a solitary, lone warrior confronting evil. Instead, it offers a unified army that vigorously and unitedly presses the battle. There is a secret weapon in our passage: Christian camaraderie, community, and esprit de corps.

Fight to the finish

Paul offers one final command: *Fight to the finish*. The ancient battle-field was a gruesome, horrific place. As two enemy phalanxes move toward each other, the decibel level increases. As they collide, the war cry and war song, the jostling of equipment on the move, mutates to what Xenophon called that "particular sound," that "awful crash," "a terrible cacophony of smashed bronze, wood, and flesh."[4] With the collision, huge clouds of dust engulf the battlefield. One brief passage from an ancient Roman battle account will illustrate: "The Batavians [Roman troops from Batavia] began to close with the enemy, striking them with the bosses of their shields, stabbing them in the face, and pushing their line uphill; thereupon the other cohorts joined with eager rivalry in cutting down all the nearest enemy. . . . Everywhere there were weapons, corpses, mangled limbs, and blood-soaked earth."[5]

Paul is adopting no tame metaphor. He imagines the church as an army suiting up and entering the fray, charging forward with full energy to that moment when the two opposing forces crash together and fight in deadly, close-order combat. The verb "to stand," used repeatedly in our passage (Ephesians 6:11, 13 [twice], 14), refers to the needed action at the awful moment of impact. Paul commands no defensive posture or mere holding action. As general, he conveys the Commander's orders for a full, zealous, fight-to-the-finish attack on evil.

We should, though, carefully note something about Paul's vigorous image of the church militant. He closely guards the meaning of the metaphor. He does not intend that we Christian soldiers should take up actual arms or be combative in our relationships within or outside of the family of God. He has surely made as much clear: "Let all bitterness and wrath and anger and clamor and slander be put away from you, along with all malice. Be kind to one another, tenderhearted, forgiving one another, as God in Christ forgave you" (Ephesians 4:31, 32). Within our passage, in a finely tuned phrase, Paul cleverly guards the meaning of the metaphor: "As shoes for your feet put on whatever will make you ready to proclaim *the gospel of peace*" (Ephesians 6:15, NRSV; emphasis added). The church's role, as someone has termed it, is to "wage peace."

In the church's battle, the weapons are not M16s and rocket launchers. Rather, the church's divinely issued weapons are truth, righteousness, readiness to proclaim a peace-filled gospel, faith, the assurance of salvation, and the Spirit-breathed Word of God. In the immediate context of our passage, the church's battle strategies include spiritual alertness in Spirit-bathed prayer all the time and for every cause, especially prayer for our fellow believers ("all the saints," verse 18) and for a bold witness to the truth of the gospel.

Moving to the wider context of the letter, we sample the church's strategies:

- "humility and gentleness" (Ephesians 4:2)
- "patience, bearing with one another in love" (verse 2)
- zealous guarding of unity (verses 3–6)
- treasuring those given by the risen Christ to His church: apostles, prophets, evangelists, and pastor-teachers (verses 11–13)
- forgiveness (verse 32)
- singing psalms, hymns, and spiritual songs (Ephesians 5:19)
- submission to one another (verse 21)

These would be strange weapons and weird strategies for any usual army. But they are just the ticket for the peace-waging army of Christ.

Paul says it best, perhaps, in 2 Corinthians 10:4, 5: "For the weapons of our warfare are not merely human, but they have divine power to destroy strongholds. We destroy arguments and every proud obstacle raised up against the knowledge of God, and we take every thought captive to obey Christ" (NRSV).

The story of Deacon Jon

Jon Pace is a FedEx finance manager and a deacon at the Germantown Church of Christ in Memphis, Tennessee. As part of his duties as deacon, he manages the computer network at his church. Given his love for math, Jon installed a background program on the church's computers that automatically searched for unknown prime numbers.

That little program churned away for fourteen years until it struck pay dirt on December 26, 2017. "There are tens of thousands of computers involved in the search," Deacon Pace comments. "The odds of one of my computers making a prime number discovery are astronomical." Early in 2018, Deacon Pace was declared the official discoverer of a rare kind of prime number, a Mersenne prime number, the fiftieth and largest ever to be found. It is 23,249,425 digits—a million digits larger than the previous record holder. It takes seventy sheets of 11" × 17" paper to print out the number in a two-point font!

As I read the news story, it was the concluding quote from Deacon Pace that caught my attention: "There were two much smaller numbers he was even prouder of: 'the 20 years I've served as a deacon at Germantown,' and 'the 44 gallons of blood . . . I've donated in my life.' "[6] Not forty-four pints, mind you; forty-four *gallons*!

Paul's ringing conclusion to Ephesians, his battle cry, asks this searching question of us: What is your blood number? As combatants in the great controversy, how much skin do we have in this fight? How much blood are we willing to spill? How eager are we to step to the front lines of the battle and throw everything into the fight? How ready are we to wage peace in the name of King Jesus? What is your blood number?

1. "British Ambassador Arrested at Tehran Demonstration," *Guardian*, US ed., January 11, 2020, https://www.theguardian.com/world/2020/jan/11/british-ambassador-arrested-at-demonstration-in-tehran-reports.

2. See especially Deuteronomy 20:5–9; Judges 7:15, 17, 18; 2 Samuel 10:11, 12; 1 Chronicles 19:12, 13; 2 Chronicles 20:15–17, 20; 32:6–8.

3. Jeffrey Asher, "Military Metaphor, Martial Values, and the Classical Battle Experience in Eph 6:10–20" (paper, Annual Meeting of the Midwest Region of the SBL/AOS/ASOR, Chicago, IL, 2000), 7.

4. Xenophon, *Cyropaedia* 7.1.35, quoted in Victor Davis Hanson, *The Western Way of War* (New York: Oxford University Press, 1989), 152, 153.

5. A. D. Lee, "Morale and the Roman Experience of Battle," in *Battle in Antiquity*, ed. Alan B. Lloyd (Swansea, Wales: Classical Press of Wales, 2009), 202.

6. Valencia Prashad, "How a Church Deacon Found the Biggest Prime Number Yet (It Wasn't as Hard as You Think)," *New York Times*, January 26, 2018, https://www.nytimes.com/2018/01/26/science/prime-number-mersenne-church.html. For details on Pace's discovery, see https://www.mersenne.org/primes/press/M77232917.html.

14

Ephesians in the Heart

Ephesians 1-6; 3:10

As we conclude our study of Ephesians, we step back into a house church assembly in ancient Ephesus, recalling that the letter was crafted to be heard in a single setting. What is the letter, taken as a whole, about? God has acted in Christ and through the Spirit to initiate His plan "to unite all things in him [Christ], things in heaven and things on earth" (Ephesians 1:10) by creating the church as "one new humanity" (Ephesians 2:15, NIV), composed of both Jews and Gentiles. In this chapter, we review the entire letter through the lens of Paul's teaching about the church. We begin with a central passage: Ephesians 3:10.

What is the church's job?

In Ephesians 3:10, Paul calls on believers to act in concert with the Father's plan for the future (Ephesians 1:9, 10) and Christ's victory on the cross (Ephesians 2:13–16). In doing so, he offers one of the most interesting and compelling descriptions of the role of the church in all of the Bible: "So that through the church the manifold wisdom of God might now be made known to the rulers and authorities in the heavenly places" (Ephesians 3:10). This job description deserves close attention.

What is the essential role of the church? The church is to be the instrument of revelation: "So that through the church the manifold wisdom of God might now be made known." The church is not self-serving. It does not go forth to proclaim a message about itself but a message about God. The church is an instrument of revelation, not the object of it.

What is the church to reveal? The church is to make known "the manifold wisdom of God." "Manifold" is the English translation of the Greek word *polupoikilos*, which means "varied," "many sided," or "multifaceted." Paul holds the glorious gem of God's plan of salvation up to the light, admiring the fresh beauty of every facet. This "multifaceted wisdom of God" is His plan to include both Jews and Gentiles as full and equal partners in His church (verses 4–6; cf. Ephesians 2:11–22). By its very composition—its unprecedented unity in great diversity—the church reveals, exhibits, and illustrates God's grand purpose to unify all things in Christ (Ephesians 1:9, 10).

To whom is the church to reveal this truth? The church is to reveal this truth "to the rulers and authorities in the heavenly places." Ephesians 1:20–23 describes these powers as subjugated to the risen and exalted Jesus, while Ephesians 6:10–20 describes them as the enemies of the church.

For what purpose? Paul does not state the purpose of the church's revelation of God's wisdom to the powers. This means we need to explore the wider letter for clues to it. Satan opposes God's grand plan to unify everything in Christ (Ephesians 1:9, 10); "the prince of the power of the air, the spirit that is now at work in the sons of disobedience" (Ephesians 2:2) and all "the rulers and authorities in the heavenly places" (Ephesians 3:10) stand in opposition to the church's efforts to proclaim God's plan, which is "the gospel of peace" (Ephesians 6:10–20; especially verse 15). The unity of the church signals the start of God's plan to unify everything. Through the church, the evil powers are put on notice that God's plan is underway and their doom assured.

God's plan to unify everything in Christ has begun and will succeed!

Metaphors for the church

As Ephesians 3:10 suggests, in composing Ephesians, Paul focuses a great deal of attention on the church. When he discusses the church (Greek, *ekklēsia*) in the letter, it is the "universal" church or the church at large rather than a local congregation.[1] A principal strategy he uses to talk about the church is to employ vibrant metaphors. (A *metaphor* is a "figure of speech whereby we speak about one thing in terms which are seen to be suggestive of another."[2]) We have watched him develop four of these metaphors in some detail: the church as a body (Ephesians 1:22, 23; 2:16; 3:6; 4:1–16, 25; 5:23, 29, 30), a building or temple (Ephesians 2:19–22), a bride (Ephesians 5:25–27), and an army (Ephesians 6:10–20). Understanding these metaphors requires attentiveness on our part because their meaning often depends upon understanding something about the first-century Greco-Roman world. We should take them seriously, examining each metaphor carefully and pondering how each functions in the context of Ephesians because they are one of the ways God communicates truth to us.[3]

The church as the body of Christ

Paul uses the "body of Christ" metaphor, which he employs in 1 Corinthians 12 and Romans 12, several times in Ephesians: Ephesians 1:22, 23; 2:16; 4:1–16; 5:29, 30. The most developed use comes in Ephesians 4:1–16, where he underscores relationships among members, emphasizing that ministers of the Word were given to the church by Christ from His position of Lordship over the cosmos.

The metaphor that the church is a body, or, more specifically, the church is the body of Christ, reminds us that healthy relationships among members and cohesion to Christ are essential for the church. Advancing knowledge of anatomy and physiology, far from rendering

Paul's use of the metaphor obsolete, has only served to heighten the impact of these points. The thrust of this metaphor "is one of activity. Christ directs, controls and energizes the members . . . so that they may serve his purpose in the world. Thus part of the church's reason for being is that *it may minister to the world as Christ's agent.*"[4]

The church as the temple of God

Paul redeploys his temple metaphor (1 Corinthians 3:9–17; 2 Corinthians 6:14–7:1) in Ephesians 2:19–22, where it functions as a culminating image for the inclusion of Gentiles as full partners in the church. Gentile and Jewish believers together form "a holy temple in the Lord" that is "being built together for a dwelling place of God in the Spirit" (verses 21, 22).

In Paul's metaphor, God is both Builder (implied) and Occupant of the structure. The foundation is "the apostles and prophets" (verse 20), the cornerstone is Christ, and the building materials consist of both Jewish and Gentile believers, with the metaphor illustrating their cohesion in the church. A number of common ideas about temples are active here, including structural integrity (a building or temple made of different materials coheres), the process of building (temples are built), and habitation (since the temple is "a dwelling in which God lives by his Spirit," verse 22, NIV).

The church as the bride of Christ

In offering counsel to Christian husbands (Ephesians 5:25–33), Paul uses the idea from the Old Testament of the people of God as His bride or wife (e.g., Hosea; Jeremiah 2; 3; 13:20–27; Ezekiel 16; 23), which he had employed earlier (2 Corinthians 11:1–4), to focus on the relationship between Christ and the church. Elements and roles of the ancient wedding ceremony are consolidated in Christ in a bid to portray all Christ does for His church.

In addition to His central role as the Groom, Christ Himself is

1. the bride price since He "gave himself up for her" (verse 25);
2. the One who administers the bridal bath: "That he might sanctify her, having cleansed her by the washing of water with the word" (verse 26); and
3. the One who presents the bride to Himself (verse 27)!

All of these stretch the boundaries of ancient wedding practices, but the resulting stress on the metaphor serves only to emphasize the importance of Christ for the church. While the passage underscores the past and present attentions of the Bridegroom toward the bride, it also offers an important element of eschatological expectation in the future "presentation" (verse 27). At that time, Christ's second coming, the full result of the Bridegroom's work will be manifested in the splendor of the bride.

The church as the militia of Christ

As we have noted, Paul had also used military metaphors earlier: Romans 13:11–14; 1 Thessalonians 5:8; 2 Corinthians 10:3–6. In Ephesians 6:10–20, he uses an extended, detailed military metaphor—the church as the army of God—to summarize and conclude the letter. The metaphor could be misunderstood as urging actual combat or combativeness, but Paul carefully guards against it through a context advocating the virtues of kindness, tenderheartedness, and forgiveness (especially Ephesians 4:17–32) and through a clarification that the church is to proclaim "the gospel of peace" (Ephesians 6:15).

Paul's military metaphor depicts the church's battle against evil as combat that requires the foe's full, sustained, and energetic engagement. Believers are not merely sentinels who stand stoically at watch but combatants (albeit in the interest of peace). The passage represents a call to arms that is especially interested in the esprit de corps of believers. It does not envision Christians (or Paul) as lone warriors, battling in splendid isolation. Instead, it portrays the church militant, in which the addressees are to enlist as fellow soldiers against the church's foes. Read in this way, the passage presents a developed metaphor for the church—the importance of which is emphasized by its climactic position in the letter. The "the church is an army" metaphor highlights, in a way other metaphors do not, the church's engagement against the forces of evil and the real struggle and suffering that such conflict entails, all the while assuring believers of the adequacy of God's provision and the victory that awaits.

Since every metaphor highlights some aspects of reality while it hides others, we are best served by valuing all these metaphors for the church and treasuring what they teach us about being part of God's plan to unify all things in Christ.[5] In the church of which you are a part, "God is building the multiracial, multiethnic, multigenerational church of Jesus Christ, which stands as a monument to his triumph over the powers of darkness" and points the way to the fulfillment of His plan to unite the cosmos in Jesus.[6]

* * * * *

Prisca and Aquila awaken, fresh from yesterday's inspiring Sabbath meeting of followers of the Way.[7] There they had heard the latest from their imprisoned friend Paul through his letter about God's actions to create the church. Paul's vivid pictures of the church come alive as they begin the week.

Making their way to their shop in the marketplace, they walk down Curetes Street. Most days they would pass the long rows of statues that line either side of the street without much thought. This morning, though, the statues evoke Paul's image of the church as a body. Pausing to admire an especially large and fine one, they remember that Christ is the Head and that they, together with all believers, are parts of Christ's own body, doing His bidding in the world.

Continuing their journey, they see in most every block a beautiful temple dedicated to the worship of some deity. The first rays of the sun splash their glory on these architectural masterpieces. Looking to the west, the two catch a distant glimpse of the Artemision, the most glorious temple of all. Prisca and Aquila are reminded, with a jolt of inspiration, that these temples point to a grand, transcendent reality of which they are honored to be part—the temple of the church of the Living God, made up not of stones but of a rich variety of people, a living temple in which God, the Creator of everything, is worshiped.

Closer to the marketplace, they see debris from a nighttime wedding procession strewn along its route and recall Paul's description of the church as the bride of Christ. As believers, followers of the Way, they are part of the bride of Christ, awaiting the most momentous wedding procession of all. Nearer still to their shop, Prisca and Aquila can see, in the mist creeping in from the bay, a training ground for the cohorts of Roman legionnaires assigned to Ephesus. They pause to watch the soldiers' early morning exercises, marching in their gear, practicing the enforcement of Pax Romana, the peace of Rome. Above the cadence-marking commands of the Roman centurions, Prisca and Aquila hear the urgent battle speech of Paul and acknowledge afresh that they are themselves well-equipped soldiers, members of a powerful peace-waging army.

By the time they arrive at their tent-making shop, they are inspired with a fresh sense of significance. Whatever this day may bring, they will live it with new zest, knowing that they are part of the body of Christ, the temple of the Living God, the bride promised to Christ, and the militia of Christ. An outsider might think of their house church assembly as a small, unimportant group with little influence or power. Prisca and Aquila know better. They and their fellow believers live lives of cosmic significance. They are the church of the Living God, tasked with exhibiting the exaltation of Christ in the streets of their city, preparing the way for His return.

---

1. Ephesians 1:22; 3:10, 21; 5:23, 24, 25, 27, 29, 32. In Paul's earlier letters, he usually had local congregations in mind. But see 1 Corinthians 10:32; 12:28; 15:9; Galatians 1:13; and Philippians 3:6, where a broader sense may be in view.

2. Janet M. Soskice, *Metaphor and Religious Language* (Oxford: Clarendon, 1985), 15.

3. See John K. McVay, "Biblical Metaphors for the Church and Adventist Ecclesiology," *Andrews University Seminary Studies* 44, no. 2 (October 2006): 285–315, especially "How to Analyze Metaphors for the Church," 288–291.

4. Ralph P. Martin, *The Family and the Fellowship: New Testament Images of the Church* (Grand Rapids, MI: Eerdmans, 1980), 123; emphasis in the original.

5. The idea that metaphors both highlight and hide is from George Lakoff and Mark Johnson, *Metaphors We Live By* (Chicago: University of Chicago Press, 1980), 10–14.

6. Timothy G. Gombis, *The Drama of Ephesians: Participating in the Triumph of God* (Downers Grove, IL: IVP Academic, 2010), 182.

7. Prisca (or Priscilla) and Aquila were friends, fellow tentmakers, and dedicated co-evangelists with Paul in Corinth (1 Corinthians 18:1–3) and Ephesus (verses 18, 19) and hosted a house church in Rome (Romans 16:3). Since 2 Timothy 4:19 places them back in Ephesus, I have used their names here.